LEGACY

The Secret History of Proto-Fascism in America's Greatest Little City

Scott Smith

This book is dedicated to the people of LaGrange, Georgia. By shining the light of reason upon our community's secret history, we may avoid repeating it.

CONTENTS

FOREWORD: THE FOUNDATION

In a discussion about historical research, a wise friend once said, "You don't slander someone's legacy. That's something you just don't do."

I respect this sentiment, and I do not want to slander anyone's legacy. It would be easy to slander by making assumptions. When looking back at history, we cannot know all the truths. We can only research, analyze, and make educated guesses that are often tenuous at best.

Yet we can learn from these informed guesses. They're not always correct, but they may begin a dialogue that leads to a better understanding of the issues at hand. And that is the purpose of this book -- to begin a dialogue.

In this book, I examine institutional racism, sexism, religious fundamentalism, and right-wing authoritarianism in LaGrange, Georgia, "America's Greatest Little City" (and my hometown). Additionally, the provocative title of this book refers to a *secret history* of proto-fascism in LaGrange. "Proto-fascism" simply means the beginning stages of fascism.

So . . . What is fascism?

I do not use the term "fascism" lightly, and I do not employ it as an insult directed at any individual(s). Fascism is a right-wing, authoritarian socio-political system that revolves around the merger of big business and government. According to Dr. Lawrence Britt, who studied the fascist regimes of Hitler (Germany), Mussolini (Italy), Franco (Spain), and others, there are 14 common, defining characteristics of fascism, including disdain for human rights, identification of the enemy as a unifying force, intertwining of religion and government, rampant sexism, protection of corporate power, and suppression of labor power. (We'll explore all of the characteristics more thoroughly in chapter seven.)

Of course, LaGrange is a little city, not a country, but there was a time not too long ago when one corporation's power grew dangerously close to fascism at the municipal level. This corporation controlled virtually everything in the city -- jobs, stores, banks, schools, churches, neighborhoods, government, press, and even the swimming pools.

During my childhood in LaGrange, there was a white swimming pool and a black swimming pool; a white library and a black library; a white recreation center and a black recreation center. This type of racial segregation was common in the 1950s and 60s throughout the South. But in LaGrange, things stayed that way until the early 1990s.

The corporate power of the Callaway Mills textile company persisted long after the cotton mills were sold to Roger Milliken in 1968. Today the Callaway Foundation, Inc. clings to the remnants of that corporate power in the form of hundreds of millions of dollars.

It was the Foundation that continued to fund racial segregation in our community after the rest of the South had moved beyond "separate but equal" facilities for blacks and whites.

To gain entrance to the whites-only swimming pool, library, or recreation center, one had to be a member of the Callaway Educational Association (CEA), a private social organization funded by the Foundation. Officially, the only way to become a member was to be asked to join by an existing member. Unofficially, all that mattered was being white. (Or, rather, all that really mattered was *not* being black, as there were a few Middle Eastern and Asian members.)

Why did Callaway Mills invest so heavily in the social engineering of our community? Why did this corporation want to control the entire social sphere of the community, including where people lived and who could swim in certain swimming pools?

Fuller E. Callaway, founder of Callaway Mills, gave the answer in a 1919 speech to fellow industrialists: "We have tickets which entitle the holder to admission [to the swimming pool]. Now, you take a doffer boy [a mill worker], and if he does not behave, we take his swimming ticket away from him, and it has more influence with him than the fear of God."[1]

If I am interpreting Mr. Callaway's paternalistic remarks correctly, then the goal of his social engineering project was to create a community of obedient, submissive workers. But why did Callaway's legacy continue to fund racial segregation until the last decade of the twentieth century? What did segregation have to do with cotton mills?

Historical facts suggest that corporate-funded segregation kept mill workers divided and conquered after the great textile strike of

1934-35. Bill Lightle describes the momentous strike in his book *Mill Daddy*:

> Readers learned from an Associated Press story that
> 200,000 textile workers had walked off their jobs because of
> low pay and abusive working conditions, including 25,000 in
> Georgia. Textiles were Georgia's largest industry, then
> employing more than 60,000 workers. Before the strike
> ended, 500,000 workers would participate nationwide.
> Georgia mill workers, briefly, thought that maybe, finally, a
> political leader was going to help them. They were wrong.
>
> Democratic Governor Eugene Talmadge's primary re-
> election was scheduled for September 12, as the strike was
> underway. He gave emotional speeches to cotton mill
> workers saying, 'I will never use the troops to break up a
> strike.' He lied.
>
> After he won the election, Talmadge ordered Georgia's
> entire National Guard of 4,000 to 'arrest the picketers and
> get the mills back in operation.' Soon union leaders were
> arrested and were not allowed to communicate with fellow
> workers. Having tricked the workers, Talmadge made the
> owners happy . . .
>
> Striking workers in Georgia had the help of United Textiles
> Workers of America and the support of President Roosevelt
> but they achieved little and endured much violence and
> death. Five Georgia mill workers were killed, including one
> beaten to death as his family watched but could not stop
> the militiamen, on Callaway Mill property near Columbus.[2]

Wow! I thought when I first read this. *Why have I never heard this story before?*

I guess it's not something that most people want to talk about. It's certainly not a nice subject for an afternoon chat over sweet tea; it's downright frightening. Before I started doing research for this book, I had heard only whispered rumors alluding to the fact that the Callaway Mills Company had once wielded the ultimate corporate power: the power to call in military forces to *kill* a working-class uprising.

The following *New York Times* article from May 13, 1935 reveals that the Callaway Mills employee who was "beaten to death as his family watched" was in fact a LaGrange resident:

> LA GRANGE, Ga., May 12 - Court-martial of two unnamed Georgia National Guardsmen has been ordered following upon the death last night of Fonie Stephens, a Callaway cotton mill striker.
>
> It also was learned today that the courts-martial by the same group of officers are to follow for nineteen strikers now detained under military arrest by the National Guard near Atlanta.
>
> Stephens, injured two weeks ago in a brush with troopers when authorities began to evict strikers from company houses, died in a hospital a few days ago.
>
> The examining physicians said he died from complications resulting from bruises on the head, but added that a weak heart might have contributed to his death.

The two soldiers were eventually acquitted of any wrongdoing after the medical examiner -- none other than Fuller E. Callaway's nephew, Dr. Enoch Callaway -- testified that Stephens had died from a skin infection, and that the bruising on his head was only a secondary cause of death.

Following the governor's orders, the state militia had ended the strike and protected the corporate interests of Georgia's cotton mill owners. In the process, they killed LaGrange resident Fonie Stephens. During the great textile strike in Georgia, militiamen also held several strikers under military arrest at an internment camp at Ft. McPherson in Atlanta.

Is this snippet of our secret history starting to sound like the beginnings of fascism? I think Mussolini would say so, based on his understanding of the term: "Fascism should more appropriately be called corporatism because it is a merger of state and corporate power."[3]

In LaGrange, there was certainly a merger of state and corporate power in 1935 -- and the fledgling Nazi Party in Germany took notice. As Governor Talmadge declared martial law and placed striking cotton mill workers into internment camps (a.k.a. concentration camps), "Newspapers in Nazi Germany crowed that this was a sign of fascism's coming global triumph."[4]

Again, I do not wish to slander anyone's legacy. I am not suggesting that Fuller E. Callaway or his successors were fascists. They're not around to answer such a charge, and besides, I don't think they were.

In the interest of full disclosure, I must admit that I was a grateful recipient of Callaway Foundation philanthropic funds in the form of the Hatton Lovejoy Scholarship. However, in the shadows of the Foundation's much-publicized philanthropy, there is a more insidious side to the Callaway cotton empire. Many people don't know this side of the story, and I think it's important for us to reconsider this unspoken history from our current vantage point.

After the great strike ended in 1935, there was no more talk of union activity in LaGrange (nothing above a whisper, at least). "Union" became a taboo word and still is today. Having witnessed the full force of the state militia terminate a human life as well as the great textile strike, Callaway Mill workers quietly went back to their "separate but equal" neighborhoods and facilities in LaGrange. In the six decades that followed, the Callaway Foundation would spend millions to maintain racial segregation.

Again -- I must stress this -- I do not wish to slander any individual's legacy, but I do have many questions about the legacy of such immense corporate power in our community. According to the Foundation's website (CallawayFoundation.org): "Since 1943, public and private institutions and programs in the fields of religion, charity and education have been greatly enhanced by gifts totaling more than $275 million. Even after such giving, assets of approximately $200 million still remain and, by asset size, the Foundation ranks 30th among the hundreds of private foundations in the southeastern United States."[5]

The Foundation seems to be proud of its large assets. Nonetheless, it sounds like a wonderful organization, right? In many ways, it is. It has done much good. As I mentioned before, I have personally benefited from its philanthropic funds, as have many educational institutions across the state. However, I have to wonder: Is this private foundation merely a benign charity that doles out money to the needy? Or is there something more to it?

INTRODUCTION: CALLAWAY'S AMERICA

"I make American citizens and run cotton mills to pay the expenses."
- Fuller E. Callaway[6]

In many ways, I am a product of the Callaway corporate system. The Callaway Foundation awarded a generous scholarship to me and contributed several thousand dollars toward my college tuition. In my hometown of LaGrange, signs of Fuller E. Callaway's influence abound. The office in which I type this sentence was built as a house for a Callaway Mills manager. The Troup County Archives Building, where I conducted research for this book, once housed the offices of Fuller E. Callaway. During the summertime I often enjoy relaxing on the beach and strolling through the beautiful landscapes of Callaway Gardens, a tourist destination near LaGrange (in Pine Mountain, Georgia) that was founded by Mr. Callaway's son Cason.

Here in Troup County, Georgia, there's a Callaway Elementary School, Callaway Middle School, Callaway High School, Callaway Church, Callaway Avenue, Callaway Church Road, Callaway Airport, Callaway Lake, and Callaway Stadium -- and this just scratches the surface of local Callaway namesakes. But this book is about neither the concrete landmarks nor the noteworthy landscapes left behind by Callaway. This book is primarily about how one corporation shaped the *psychological* landscape of our community for the

1

greater part of the twentieth century; it is about how the Callaway Mills Company cultivated generations of obedient mill workers through oppressive social engineering projects such as the funding of institutional racism and religious fundamentalism.

As Mr. Callaway said, he made American citizens. *Indeed!*

This book explores Callaway's America and the secret history of our community. The idea for this book began to coalesce in a journal entry that I wrote for a Social Psychology class in 2010. In the entry I described my own childhood experience with institutional racism at the Callaway Educational Association (CEA), the renowned, whites-only (or, more accurately, "no blacks") social club in LaGrange.

The following personal story is both mind-blowing and shameful for me. I was a member of this openly racist and discriminatory institution as late as 1990. As a 10-year-old at the time, I didn't know any better. I should have. It's not as if the institutional discrimination was subtle -- it was blatantly obvious -- yet it was unspoken and seemed to be accepted by everyone in the community. That's just the way it was in LaGrange, and I knew of nothing else.

The main building of the CEA was essentially a recreation center for light-skinned children. It was founded in 1944 as an educational institution for children of Callaway Mills employees.[7] Even though the Callaway family sold the textile company to Milliken in 1968, the CEA remained in operation as a private club and staple of the community. The CEA encompassed a swimming pool, recreation center, auditorium, gymnasium, sports fields, and library. To be fair, the Callaway Foundation also built a recreation center and pool for black residents on the other side of town ("The LaGrange Foundation for Negroes"), but the facilities were smaller and had fewer resources in comparison to the facilities for whites. No surprise there. *Were "separate but equal" facilities ever really equal?*

During my childhood, there was also a municipal pool in LaGrange that permitted the entrance of blacks and whites (and other races, too, I presume). I remember that my little league baseball teams had to host end-of-season pool parties at the city pool so that all team members could attend. Although I made a few trips to the city pool, I spent more time at the CEA pool. I took swimming lessons there as a young child, and so did my parents. There weren't any "No Blacks Allowed!" signs posted -- but everyone knew. I never saw anybody get kicked out of the pool or any CEA facilities; however, a friend of mine remembers some kids getting kicked out of the pool area for "trying to pass." Their skin was just a little too dark. I wonder what the lifeguard said to them. *Sorry, kids, you're just not quite white enough!*

New CEA members had to be "sponsored" (*not black*) to receive a membership card. I remember getting a membership card as a child so that I could visit the library and play basketball in the gym, both of which were within walking distance of my father's office. As far as I remember, I was never officially invited or "sponsored," but I was white, and they gave me a card. No questions asked.

I remember being proud of my membership card. *I was a member!* At the time, it didn't seem like I was supporting institutional racism or joining a club akin to the KKK. I just wanted to play basketball and check out library books. After all, children of the wealthiest, most prominent families in LaGrange were members of the CEA. That's just the way it was.

I didn't see anything wrong with being a member of the CEA until an eye-opening event that occurred when I was about 10-years-old. When I walked outside after playing air hockey at the CEA rec center, a black woman in the parking lot asked me if I could go back inside and find the girl she was babysitting. I almost asked, "Why can't you do it?"

Then it hit me -- and suddenly it all seemed so wrong. I could see the shame in the woman's eyes for having to ask me, a child, to help her with such a simple task. I knew that it was wrong for her to feel shame, and so I felt shame, too. I don't remember going back to the CEA after that encounter. I hope I didn't.

The CEA existed up until 1993, when the Callaway Foundation donated most of the CEA property to LaGrange College. It may be hard for you to believe that such an openly racist institution lasted for so long. It's hard for *me* to believe, and I was a card-carrying member.

I always knew there was something a little strange about LaGrange. I suspected that it might have something to do with all the churches. For most of my life, there were more churches than restaurants in the city. When I started doing research for this book, I discovered *why* there are so many churches in LaGrange. I also learned about the links between racism, sexism, authoritarianism, fundamentalism, and submission in the workplace. I learned how the Cotton King divided and conquered -- and how the working people fought amongst themselves rather than uniting against their oppressor. And I discovered that the cotton mill workers in LaGrange *did* actually break down racial barriers and unite against their common oppressor for a few weeks in 1935. Of course, their effort ended with the brutal killing of a man by state soldiers. I wondered why I had never heard this story before. It's a story worth telling. It may hurt at times, but people need to know the truth.

CHAPTER ONE: KING COTTON

King Cotton ruled West Georgia long before Fuller E. Callaway became the Cotton King. Eli Whitney invented the modern cotton gin in 1793, and Georgia's slave-powered plantation economy bloomed. By the early 1800s, plantations had spread to West Georgia, which was still controlled by the Muscogee Native Americans, commonly known as Creek Indians.

The Creek Nation had been generally cooperative with settlers from Europe. In a mutually beneficial business arrangement, the colonists shipped in slaves from Africa while the Creeks captured slaves in Florida (Seminole Native Americans). Creeks and settlers traded slaves as well as goods like animal skins and textiles. As the plantation economy spread across Georgia, plantation owners attempted to assimilate the Creek Nation into their system. Many Creeks did not like the idea of assimilation – but the Europeans had already begun to assimilate through other means: procreation.

William McIntosh was the son of a Creek mother named Senoia and a wealthy Scottish father. McIntosh was raised as a Creek Indian and eventually became chief of the Creek Nation. The Creeks believed that ancestry was passed on through the mother;

therefore, they weren't too concerned that McIntosh's father was a white man. Although McIntosh never met his father, he kept in touch with his paternal family and learned the ways of white culture. Because of his bloodline and his unique position, McIntosh was called upon by the white settlers to quash the Creek Indian War that broke out in 1812. After the war, he adopted the lifestyle of his father's family and built a large plantation in West Georgia. He owned 72 slaves.[8]

McIntosh's first cousin George Troup was elected governor of Georgia in 1823. Troup came from a family of plantation owners and likely saw the Creek Indians as a hindrance to progress. With the promise of protection from his cousin in the governor's mansion, Chief McIntosh signed the Treaty of Indian Springs in 1825, giving virtually all Creek land to the state of Georgia for a sum of $200,000. Soon thereafter McIntosh was murdered at his home by angry Creeks who felt that he had betrayed his people.[9] But Troup had already gotten what he wanted, and he began to forcefully evict the Native Americans from Georgia.

Notably, a Creek Council led by Opthle Yohola argued that the Treaty of Indian Springs was fraudulent, and President John Quincy Adams agreed. President Adams nullified the Treaty of Indian Springs with the Treaty of Washington (1826). Historian R. Douglas Hurt commented, "The Creeks had accomplished what no Indian nation had ever done or would do again -- achieve the annulment of a ratified treaty."[10] Unfortunately, their diplomatic efforts proved fruitless. Governor Troup ignored the annulment and continued to evict the Native Americans, even after President Adams threatened to send in the federal troops. Troup called in his own state militia, and President Adams backed down, fearing a civil war. The

President told colleagues that "the Indians are not worth going to war over."[11]

A large portion of the land vacated by the Creek Indians officially became Troup County in 1826. By 1827, there were no more Creek Indians in Georgia.

In 1830, President Andrew Jackson's Indian Removal Act would eliminate the remaining Native Americans in Georgia, the Cherokees of North Georgia, some of whom were likely my ancestors. They were rounded up, herded into concentration camps, and forced to march thousands of miles to Oklahoma along what they called the "Nunna daul Tsuny," or Trail of Tears. Legend has it that Cherokee mothers cried so much that their tears spawned a new flower: the Cherokee Rose. To this day, the Cherokee Rose remains the official state flower of Georgia.[12]

With the Native Americans out of the way, cotton mills popped up all over Georgia, and cotton production remained the state's primary industry throughout the Civil War. In the plantation system, most slaves were provided with a little food and roofs over their heads – just enough to get by. Of course, the Civil War and subsequent abolition of slavery created a problem for plantation owners. Who would do all the work? Wealthy industrialists in the South needed a new system of slavery. Who could they exploit next? It soon became clear that children were an easy target.

Samuel Slater, known as "the father of the American Factory System," not only brought British textile manufacturing to New England but also introduced the concept of the mill village to American industrialists. Slater hired entire families and built whole villages to provide labor for his mills. The majority of Slater's mill workers were children. Children as young as age seven (and probably even younger) were exploited as cheap laborers. Of course, Slater had to keep all those children in line. Children who misbehaved or worked too slowly were sent to the "whipping room."[13]

Slater was also known as "the Father of the Sunday School System," in which young workers learned to read the Bible, say their prayers, and conform to their employer's expectations. Slater's mill villages provided working-class families with a conservative education, a roof over their heads, and just enough money to get by. In many ways, this system was not much different from slavery or serfdom. It was a different kind of slavery.

* * *

Meanwhile, back in Troup County, Fuller Earle Callaway was born to Reverend Abner Reeves Callaway and Sarah Jane Howard in 1870.[14] Like Callaway's grandfather, Reverend Enoch Callaway, Callaway's father was a Baptist minister and slave plantation owner. In 1860 Callaway's father owned 20 slaves (ranging in age from 2 to 65) at his plantation near Greenville, Georgia.[15] All of the Callaway slaves escaped from the plantation in 1864 when they heard that Atlanta had fallen to the Union army. The Reverend set out in a horse-drawn buggy to reclaim his property. He caught up with the slaves near Griffin, Georgia, put them on an auction block, and sold them for two trunks full of Confederate cash. He used that money to buy 100 bales of cotton and some land in Troup County.[16]

Legend has it that Fuller E. Callaway started selling spools of thread to rural housewives in Troup County at the age of 8 or 10. He landed his first steady job at Bradfield's Clothing Company as a delivery boy, but he quit when he was told to make a delivery to a black barber in town. However, at the time, young Fuller was living with his older brother Dr. Enoch Callaway, a successful physician who demanded "honest work" from his little brother.[17] Callaway went back to Bradfield's, asked for his job back, and eventually saved up enough money to start his own business.[18]

At age 18 he opened his first store in LaGrange. It was a five and ten cents store inspired by Woolworth's in New York. It would later become the Callaway Department Store. A shrewd businessman, Callaway invested in LaGrange's first modern cotton mill in 1895.[19] In 1900, he and several associates opened Unity Cotton Mill in LaGrange.[20] Carleton Wood, Executive Director of Hills & Dales Estate (the Callaway mansion in LaGrange) explained how Unity Mill eventually became Callaway Mills:

> It was called Unity because a group of local investors led by the Callaway, Truitt, and Dunson families unified their capital to create a completely new enterprise. Unity Mill produced cotton duck, a canvas like fabric that was used for sails, bags, tents, awnings and numerous other products. In Troup County, Unity Mill was followed by Elm City Cotton Mill, Park Cotton Mill, Unity Spinning Mill, Dunson Cotton Mill, Hillside Cotton Mill, Rockweave Cotton Mill, Stark Mill, Valley Waste Mills, Oakleaf Mills, and Valway Rug Mills. Between 1900 and 1930, the cotton mill industry would completely dominate the local scene.

> During his lifetime Callaway's enterprises grew from 0 to over 115,000 spindles, a common measure of textile manufacturing capacity. This tremendous growth made the Callaway group of companies one of the largest cotton processing centers in Georgia. They utilized the selling agents in New York J. H. Lane & Company to distribute their cotton products near and far, resulting in an almost continuously growing market for the Callaway products.

Employees, including older children, worked in large cavern-like buildings for long hours and modest pay, in frequently less than ideal conditions. Employees running the looms and other mill equipment knew all too well the repetitive sound of a cotton mill humming at full speed. For some mill workers, this humming became melodious and comforting. It represented steady wages for the workers and wealth for the mill owners.[21]

Fuller E. Callaway compared the textile boom to a disease (albeit a profitable disease) and explained how the mill owners auctioned off management positions:

It was like the measles in the South in those days. Every town wanted to build a cotton mill. We got it in LaGrange. We did not have much of anything, but we got up a cotton mill; and auctioned off the directorships. Anybody that would take $5,000 worth of stock, we would make a director; and if a widow with a son had $2,000, we would make the son a bookkeeper. We organized our little mill, and got our home people there to work in it, and we worked it along rather human lines. Everybody was proud of it and carried everything he had in it. A good many of the laborers took stock in it. We had a great many poor white people with the highest type of morality and religion. They could not produce cotton at five cents a pound against the negro; and these men began to move to town as cotton mill operatives. Their position in the country had been so poor, on account of the low price of their product, that it elevated them even to bring them to town to work in a cotton mill, which in itself was a poorly-paid occupation.[22]

Callaway's attitude toward his operatives, or employees, is a central issue in this chapter. In many ways, Callaway's treatment of his employees was considered progressive for his time. He gave them access to health care, education, and even profit sharing plans. At Christmas, he gave out bonuses, candy, and hams. Callaway essentially built a whole new town (Southwest LaGrange) for his operatives, as Carleton Wood explained:

> With all the new mills popping up in town, the population of the city boomed and the mill employees needed places to live. In LaGrange, the population exploded during the cotton mill fever years growing from 4,200 citizens in 1900, to over 18,250 in 1920, and over 20,000 citizens by 1933. Fuller Callaway Sr. and other mill leaders in LaGrange believed that if the employees of the mills were comfortable and had high quality amenities, they would be loyal and productive employees. As a result, he and other owners provided their operatives attractive mill villages. Similar housing benefits were provided to the mill's overseers; they were given larger, more substantial houses, reflecting the industrial hierarchy.

> Fuller Callaway Sr. and his mills incorporated a completely new town called Southwest LaGrange in 1917. This became necessary because the city of LaGrange was not willing to annex a proposed new mill village that was outside of the city limits, due to the cost of new infrastructure. Thanks to Fuller Callaway, Southwest LaGrange had a wide variety of public services including parks, schools, health care facilities, recreation amenities, street lights, and attractive streetscapes. Callaway ensured that Southwest LaGrange was successful and won much devotion from employees for

providing a livable community. In 1920 LaGrange extended its city limits from a one to two mile radius. Southwest LaGrange was incorporated into LaGrange, along with Dunson Cotton Mills east of LaGrange.

Several of my friends have said, "LaGrange wouldn't be on the map without Callaway." That may be true. Donna Jean Whitley agrees in her 1984 Ph.D. dissertation: "Without his leadership, undoubtedly much of present-day LaGrange would not exist, or at any rate would appear today in a radically different form."[23] People often speak of Fuller Callaway as if he were a folk hero who grew from humble beginnings as a boy selling spools into the ultimate community provider and patriarch, a sort of god-king.

But, in reality, Callaway was no folk hero. He was a businessman, and his gifts to the people of LaGrange were first and foremost business investments. Remember what he said about the community swimming pool? ("If [a doffer boy] does not behave, we take his swimming ticket away from him, and it has more influence with him than the fear of God.")

Although Callaway ran his mills "along rather human lines," he seemed to think of his operatives as cows. His property. His chattel.

Callaway proudly spoke about his employees' benefits at the First Industrial Conference in Washington D.C. in 1919:

> Now, at our little place, at LaGrange, we organized these mills, and the first thing we started was a school, and I had one old-fashioned director of the old type, that objected. He said, 'What do you mean by building a school to educate these people, and then not be able to control them after being educated?' Well, I took the position that an educated man was like a cow -- and I wish to say here that I use cows often for my illustrations. With my own cows, I get good

blooded stock, because they do not eat any more than scrubs, I give them a nice house, curry them, and then rub them on the nose before milking, and they give 4 gallons of cream. And a cow is better off for giving 4 gallons than letting her get in somebody's blueberry patch, getting full of ticks, and only giving a pint of milk.[24]

Callaway went on to explain why he also provided health care for his employees:

The next thing we started on was a hospital to care for the health of the people. It is, I assure you, a perfectly practicable thing. Before we got the hospital these people who came out of the mountains -- good Anglo-Saxons, the best people in the world, who had spent their lives in the mountains for centuries and have not been polluted by living in cities like you men have -- well, anyhow, before that these people had no idea of hygiene or science or caring for their health, or anything like that. They had been used to going rabbit hunting, living 20 or 15 in a house and having big families, unless, perchance, the chimney fell down and killed them off -- and making bad moonshine liquor. The fact of the matter was they could not haul enough corn to town to feed the calf, but if they could make it into liquor, and make a little money out of it, that was a perfectly natural thing for them to do.

Now, when they got down to the cotton mills in a town where it was congested, they had no idea how to take care of themselves from the standpoint of health. When they would get sick, the whole family would stay out and nurse them -- they were good religious people with plenty of sentiment -- and as a result, your mill would shut down, and by the time the fellow would get convalescent and feeling good, they would feed him some sausage, and he would die, and the burial expenses would amount to $400 or $500, and they would be that much behind, so that would rob you of all the efficient services of the entire family.

To avoid being robbed of his efficient services when someone died, Callaway built a hospital and charged his employees $6 a week for access to health care services.

The Review commented on Callaway's speech at the industrial conference: "Mr. Callaway is a capitalist of a rather unusual sort. He is at the head of a group of cotton mills at LaGrange where about 7,000 operatives are employed. He believes in a closed shop; that is, closed against union labor. He has never allowed his people to be unionized. Mr. Callaway twice used the cow by way of illustration. He seemed very much impressed by that fact that she could be milked."[25]

According to the Fuller E. Callaway Foundation: "Outside observers saw what the programs at the mills were doing and, recognizing Mr. Callaway's leadership, they called him a philanthropist.

"'Philanthropist, nothing!' he said. 'I'm a businessman.'"[26]

Indeed.

Callaway seemed to control every aspect of his employees' lives. He not only controlled their livelihood but, in many cases, their homes, schools, churches, recreation centers, stores, and banks. By 1916, Callaway owned stock in several cotton mills as well as three local banks and two stores.[27]

"The company's wishes prevail in every phase of the life of the people who live in subjection under a complete industrial feudalism," author James Myers writes of the Southern textile industry. "This feudalism may be paternal and kindly. It usually is so until the authority is questioned or its will is threatened by a show of independence on the part of the workers . . . In such industrial cases, the entire machinery of autocracy goes into action. The workers are evicted from their houses, intimidated by police, or deported from town."[28]

Callaway ruled over LaGrange as a sort of feudal overlord, and this meant that his employees *had* to be obedient and loyal. Otherwise, he could ruin their entire lives -- and he was not above making such threats. He thought of his business as the goose that laid the golden eggs, and he often reminded people of his unique position. And nothing seemed to threaten his position more than the possibility of union organization.

Thus, in July 1920, as unions became more popular throughout the country, the LaGrange Chamber of Commerce financed an extensive anti-union advertising campaign which revolved around the following declaration: "For the best interests of LaGrange and her people we oppose the organization of labor unions in LaGrange."[29]

The newly created LaGrange Chamber of Commerce was launched by Callaway with the primary intention of campaigning against unions. Of course, Callaway himself was a member of the Chamber. His secretary, Ab Perry, was also Secretary of the Chamber, and most Chamber correspondence originated directly from the Callaway General Offices. These facts, along with "the amount and content of correspondence in the Callaway files relating to this subject make it clear that Fuller Callaway was the moving force behind much of the drive."[30]

The Chamber hired a PR firm in Atlanta to manage the anti-union campaign, which included several opinion pieces from the

Chamber itself as well as prominent citizens, religious leaders, and businessmen.[31] According to the Chamber, "That the people of LaGrange are practically unanimous in their determination that labor unions shall not find a place in this city is demonstrated by the declaration to this effect which was circulated recently, and which was signed by over 4,000 white citizens and heads of families, representing every interest in LaGrange."

(What about the interests of black citizens? Oh, yeah, right -- they didn't count!)

"Who profits by the labor union, even for a time?" another advertisement asked. "It is the employee who will give as little as he can do for as much as he can get."

"Suppose the Dunsons, the Truitts, the Callaways had been pulled down to the level of the union member, the cog in the big wheel, the level of the un-ambitious. There would have been no mills built by those men, no banks established, no great industries offering opportunity to thousands who want their change to succeed. Every doffer boy in a LaGrange mill has his chance to be superintendent. It is up to his own energy, ability, loyalty. Would a labor union help that doffer boy to become superintendent?"

(From Callaway's own explanation of why he built the community swimming pool, we know that he had his own efficient system of motivation for doffer boys, and he certainly didn't want a union to come in and ask that he no longer withhold the boys' swimming pool tickets.)

The anti-union ads went on, page after page. Here's another excerpt: "If you would know what union labor means when it shows its teeth, read the daily newspapers -- not the editorials, which express opinions, but the news columns, which record the facts. Railway systems tied up; freight yards congested, freights delayed until their value is sacrificed. Dynamite, violence, disorder -- and death! For the IWW, the Red and Bolshevik follow in the wake of the labor union. Do you want all these in LaGrange? Well, you will have them as surely as unionism gets a foothold here. The home folks of LaGrange will organize no labor unions. Outsiders will not be permitted to do so."

"Dynamite, violence, disorder -- and death!"

Damn. I guess that was a strong incentive to keep the unions out of town.

Mill manager S.H. Dunson referred to unions as "the silent, slimy, and treacherous monster in sheep's clothing that is masked under the dignified name of the American Federation of Labor" and warned that union organization would turn LaGrange into "a veritable Hell on Earth."[32]

Chamber of Commerce board member E.B. Clark reminded people that it was Callaway and other mill owners who laid the golden eggs: "Our great manufacturing industries work like brothers together, building fine school buildings, giving free education to all alike, free parks, YMCA buildings, in fact everything that goes to make life worth living, including good wages; and if business has been good at the end of the year they throw in some more for good measure."

W.P. Cofield served as the pastor at Unity Baptist Church (and, like most local pastors, he was likely on Callaway's payroll). In the Chamber of Commerce campaign, Cofield conjured up images of Jesus Christ to preach against unions. According to Cofield, Jesus demanded loyal, anti-union mill workers: "The Law of Jesus Christ must become our code of national life . . . The Law of Christ obeyed will cause the employed to respect their obligation to the employer and the community . . . Let us as the industrial people of the

17

community, apply the laws and principles of Jesus Christ in the mills by giving faithful, honest service, and in the community by living clean, wholesome, Christian lives."

But not everyone in LaGrange was anti-union. Reverend T.D. Bateman of First Presbyterian Church refused to participate in the campaign, saying he had been a "pretty careful student" of the American labor situation and his views would "hardly permit my writing the kind of article you are looking for at the time."[33]

Similarly, in a letter to the local newspaper, Reverend T.F. Malone pointed out the irony in the fact that mill owners claimed to do everything for the benefit of employees but threatened to close down the mills if employees organized. Closing down the mills in response to worker organization would certainly not be in the best interest of employees.[34]

Callaway himself penned a long anti-union advertorial in which he made it clear that he would take his golden eggs elsewhere if union organization occurred in LaGrange:

> Having been born here in LaGrange and expecting to remain here the rest of my life, I naturally feel a deep interest in anything affecting the welfare of our home town and its people. I am glad, therefore, that our people have so overwhelmingly declared against permitting our city to become cursed with labor unionism as it has unhappily been perverted in recent years under selfish, designing leadership.
>
> Labor unionism and the evils following in its truth, such as IWW-ism, Bolshevism, etc., stand indicted today before the bar of decent opinion as a most lamentable perversion of originally wholesome purposes. The human instinct for organization is strong. Man is a social being, loving contacts

with his fellows. The earlier organizations of manual workers -- guilds, as they were called -- were for the worthy purpose of service, of developing great skill among members and maintaining high standards of proficiency. But unhappily in recent years they have become distorted into instruments of selfishness, tyranny and lawless oppression . . .

In a country dedicated to the ideals of equality and opportunity for all, they seek to set up an oligarchy superior to the law itself, under which apprentices are limited, production restricted, free and independent workers subjected to every form of abuse and even maltreatment and murder, and under which the ambitions and industrious are held down to the level of the least capable and ambitious. It is simply a case of drunkenness with power, of ambitions run mad . . .

We have no military system in our businesses, no castes or classes, but all are workers, each selected for peculiar fitness for the particular work to be done. This being an age of specialization, in which one group of workers exchange the products of their labors for the things produced by workers in other lines, it is incumbent upon us all to play the game fairly with our fellow men . . .

Instead of permitting an element of antagonism to enter in our relations, we strive to make our companies, each one, like a big, happy family, each worker giving a fair day's work for a fair day's pay; and any radical departure from this principle of equal justice will simply mean the death of business, or 'killing the goose that lays the golden eggs' for us all.

I am now about to make a statement which it pains me even to consider. It is this: If by any unhappy circumstance LaGrange should be so unfortunate to become union-ridden, I am sure it would mean the death of enterprise in our fair city. Owners of capital, those who have saved and denied themselves to get ahead in the world, will not put their money where there is to be strife and division. Capable managers cannot be employed for work under such conditions. It would simply mean that no other industries would be built and that possibly that which we already have would languish.

I hope and believe that the good people of LaGrange will continue to stand united against the common enemy and prevent this plague from gaining a foothold in our midst.

Yours truly, Fuller E. Callaway

To make sure everyone got the point, Callaway posted the following notice in all of his mills: "Employees continuing in our employ do so with the agreement between us and each of them that they are not members of labor unions and that they will not become members of a textile or labor union while in our employment." He also secured personally signed pledges from each employee.[35]

In his letter to the people of LaGrange, Callaway linked unions and Bolshevism. This "red scare" tactic of tying union activity to Communism was common throughout the twentieth century and continues today. As Whitley pointed out, Callaway knew that "behind everything was LaGrange's fear, shared by much of the nation, that unions and organized labor and strikes and all that they represented were merely tools of Bolsheviks designed not to help

American workers gain a better life, but to make them subjects of a Communist state."[36]

Callaway described unions in black-and-white moral terms, as if he were a general prepping his troops for battle: unions were the evil common enemy, the plague, selfish oppressors, un-ambitious and yet overly ambitious, drunk with power, and un-American. Fuller E. Callaway, an industrialist who owned an Italian-style mansion upon a hill overlooking the town that he built, accused the unions of "seeking to set up an oligarchy superior to the law itself" in which workers were "subjected to every form of abuse and even maltreatment and murder."

Fifteen years later, Callaway Mill workers formed a union because they felt that they were being abused, mistreated, and underpaid. Under FDR's New Deal, they thought they had the right to collective bargaining.

They were wrong.

In Callaway's 1920 letter to the people of LaGrange, he wrote that "we have no military system in our businesses." Fifteen years later, however, Callaway Mills would have the full force of the state military to combat unions. In 1935, under martial law, Callaway mill workers were "subjected to every form of abuse and even maltreatment and murder."

When union organization came to Callaway Mills, what followed, as had been predicted by the Chamber of Commerce fifteen years earlier, was "dynamite, violence, disorder -- and death!" And when the smoke cleared, there was no need for the Chamber of Commerce to say, "See, we told you so." Everyone got the message. Union activity in LaGrange did indeed lead to violence, disorder, and death.

In a instance of ominous foreshadowing, a 1920 editorial cartoon in the LaGrange newspaper showed a mill worker lying face-down in a pool of his own blood outside of a cotton mill.[37] A brick beside his head was labeled "strike violence." His wife and daughter were pictured in the background, crying and screaming as they looked upon the horrific spectacle -- just as Fonie Stephens' family had watched as he was bludgeoned to death during the strike of 1935. Of course, Stephens was not killed by strikers; he was killed by soldiers who were protecting the interests of Callaway.

Fuller E. Callaway died in 1928. His sons Fuller Junior and Cason had already taken over his business a few years earlier. The Callaway Memorial, an obelisk-shaped clock tower, was erected in the middle of LaGrange's mill villages in 1929. It's still there today, surrounded by acres of meticulously landscaped grounds, towering above the crumbling mill homes as a giant phallic symbol, signifying Callaway's lasting corporate power.

CHAPTER TWO: THE LINTHEADS' LEGACY

Linthead: *A derogatory term for an employee of a textile mill, particularly in the Hill Country of the American South.*[38]

The stock market crash of 1929 sent America reeling into the Great Depression. When Franklin D. Roosevelt ran for President in 1932, he said, "I pledge you, I pledge myself, to a new deal for the American people."

FDR won the election and kept his word. His New Deal to revive the economy included the National Industrial Recovery Act (NIRA), passed in 1933, which set minimum wages and permitted workers to organize unions.[39] While unions were common in the North before the passage of NIRA, most mill workers in the South had never been allowed to organize. After NIRA, Southern textile workers felt as if they had the support of the president, and many of them went on strike to protest the "stretch-out," a system that demanded more work in less time.

In the 1934 General Textile Strike, 170,000 mill workers from Alabama to North Carolina joined together in the largest strike in the South's history. By this time, many textile mill workers had automobiles, and "flying squadrons" of vehicles drove from mill to mill, spreading news of the strike and encouraging other workers to join the United Textile Workers (UTW). Inspired by the NIRA as well as FDR's speeches in support of worker's rights, the strikers demanded an end to the stretch-out. Mill workers who couldn't keep up were fired, and the Great Depression was a bad time to get laid off. Violence erupted at several mills, including Chiquola Mill in Honea Path, South Carolina, where seven union members were shot and killed on September 6, 1934, a day that would come to be known as "Bloody Thursday."[40]

Janet Irons, author of *Testing the New Deal*, describes the "groundswell" of union activity: "The election of Franklin Roosevelt and the inauguration of the New Deal legitimized -- even in southern communities -- textile workers' open affiliation with a national union. The passage of the famous Section 7(a) of the National Recovery Act of 1933, granting workers the right to join a union free from interference from employers, would stimulate a groundswell of union participation on a scale not seen in the United States since the end of the First World War."[41]

In Georgia, Governor Eugene Talmadge effectively ended the strike on September 17, 1934 when he declared martial law. Strikes in North Carolina and South Carolina had already been shut down by their respective National Guard troops. Despite pleas from mill owners, Talmadge didn't send in the troops immediately. He had to wait until he was re-elected. (Of course.) Irons explains:

> Talmadge was running for re-election on Wednesday, September 12, and he wanted the support of the state's textile workers. Responding to numerous mill owners' requests, Talmadge replied that 'no giant corporation or big interest will ever dictate to me what to do while I am the

Governor.' Because of his stand, many textile workers supported the governor in his bid for re-election. Some even helped campaign for him. When the election came, Talmadge won by a landslide vote.

On the Friday before the election, however, the governor had met with leaders of the most important Georgia textile firms and accepted a $20,000 campaign contribution in return for the promise that he would call out the National Guard after the election was over. Over the weekend, secret preparations were made to deploy the troops the following week. Following the election, Talmadge declared a state of martial law and announced that the National Guard would be sent to the strike zone. Over the next several days, four thousand troops were dispatched in what one student of the subject has called 'the largest peacetime mobilization in the state's history.' In the most celebrated troop action, the National Guard arrested sixteen women and 112 men near Newnan, Georgia, along the western border of the state in the Chattahoochee Valley. They were taken to Fort McPherson near Atlanta and placed in an outdoor camp with a barbed wire fence that was later used to house German prisoners of war during World War II. The prison site has since achieved legendary status in textile lore as a 'concentration camp' for the textile workers.[42]

Federated Press reported that a commander at the "concentration camp" ordered soldiers to "terrorize the strikers."[43] One Atlanta journalist warned that the state of Georgia, "following the development of martial law, shooting down of strikers, and concentration camps during the strike, [was] coming forward as the spearhead of actual fascism in the U.S."[44] And even Nazi newspapers in Germany praised the fascist movement in Georgia, calling it "a sign of fascism's coming global triumph."[45]

***

The strike had been an utter failure, crushed under the jackboots of state soldiers, and morale seemed to be at an all-time low among textile workers. In Hogansville, a small city 10 miles north of LaGrange, striker Etta Mae Zimmerman called Talmadge a "dishonorable governor" for lying to textile workers. When the strike ended, Zimmerman said that textile workers "were in worse conditions than before the strike on account of union activities."[46]

You may be wondering: Where was President Roosevelt, the author of the New Deal, during the general strike? Believe it or not, there's a good chance that he was being entertained by Cason Callaway. Irons reveals: "On occasion, Roosevelt reportedly relaxed at 'the magnificent country home of Cason Callaway,' owner of Callaway Mills in LaGrange. One is left with the impression that the president did not believe [the mill owners] to be capable of the kind of cruelty that workers spoke of when they talked about the stretch-out and discrimination. No doubt the president believed such practices existed, but in his mind they could not have been as widespread as the union was claiming."[47]

Historian James J. Lorence also points to "the president's personal relationships with some Georgia mill owners" as a detrimental factor in the textile workers' failed strike.[48] Lorence continues, "Acutely aware of the critical role played by state governors and the National Guard in suppressing the strikes, UTW's Francis Gorman, chairman of the national strike committee, implored President Roosevelt and the governors, including Talmadge, to halt the use of state militias against strikers. Gorman charged that the current tactics were 'wholly unlawful' and 'provocative of disorder and deaths.' To the union it was clear that 'the principal function of these troops [was] to protect strike breakers' and thereby weaken the strike."[49]

FDR, however, did not intervene. When the strike ended, he called on mill hands to go back to work. Unfortunately, virtually everyone who went on strike no longer had a job. Callaway Mills employees who went on strike had to sign "'legal release of employment' forms and 'submit themselves to immediate eviction' [from company-owned mill village houses] lest they be denied [strike] relief."[50]

Few Callaway Mills employees participated in the general strike of 1934. Those who did were evicted from their homes, blacklisted, and locked out. The mills closed down for a couple of weeks, but there were no major demonstrations or picket lines. State troops were sent into town for a brief time, but there are no records of violence or rioting.

Bill Woodham, a weaver at Hillside Mill in LaGrange, said of the 1934 general strike: "There was no antagonism nowhere on each side, you know. The mill just closed down like you were taking a vacation or something other. We'd get out here and go to church, or go to prayer meetings, this, that, and the other. There wasn't nothing to do."[51]

Indeed, the general strike seemed like an extended vacation for most textile workers in LaGrange. There was a parade in downtown LaGrange when the strike ended and the mills re-opened.

Although the general strike ended in September 1934 and didn't affect life for most folks in LaGrange, Callaway Mill workers would soon organize a massive strike to protest the so-called "Bedaux system." Jesse Maddox, who was personnel supervisor at Dunson Mill in 1934, explained the Bedaux system: "What they do is they put the time-study men in there with stopwatches and a paper and forms, and they indicated all the different parts of that job, everything they had to do, and they measured the time it took, you know. They set that thing up there where you may, if you got a certain amount of production, you know you had a certain amount for standard there, you was, you was supposed to make that to get your base pay, and if you made more than that, you got more than that. They would call it premium."[52]

The Bedaux system meant that many people would lose their jobs, and when Callaway Mills enacted the system in 1935 (only a few months after the general textile strike of 1934), thousands of employees walked out of the mills in protest. Irons, author of *Testing the New Deal*, chronicles the 1935 strike in LaGrange:

> On March 1 [1935] approximately two thousand workers in six Callaway mills in western Georgia walked off their jobs to protest the implementation of the 'Bedaux' system, a particularly harsh form of scientific management. The Callaway management had attempted to implement this time and motion study during the summer of 1934, but had backed off as momentum for the general strike increased. Now, in March 1935, the management apparently felt confident that it could succeed. The move threatened to eliminate as many as one thousand jobs.
>
> UTW leaders threw the union's whole resources behind the Callaway Mills strike. [UTW Vice President Francis Gorman] called the dispute 'the most serious situation since the September strike' and a 'test case' for the implementation of the stretch-out across the South . . .
>
> For nearly eight weeks the union held out while appealing to the [Textile Labor Relations Board] for a decision. But

they could not last forever: the strikers included only about two-thirds of the workforce, and Governor Talmadge had again called in the state militia. When the mill began evicting strikers near the end of April, desperate workers petitioned the federal government to do something. Finally, on May 11, the TLRB handed down its decision on the controversy. But the ruling could not have been worse for the strikers; the new work system was completely legitimized.

Gorman understood only all too well what had happened. 'I feel that this decision forms the climax of a long line of decisions,' he said after the ruling was issued . . . The TLRB had given the mill 'a clean bill of health to go and sin some more. Not only that, the Board has run up the signal to all southern mills to go to it and smash standards all the way.' By the end of the spring of 1935, Gorman was denouncing the TLRB as a 'strikebreaking agency' . . .

Any hope that textile unionists had was now dashed. By the end of May 1935, President Green of the [American Federation of Labor] reported that wage cuts were taking place 'in every direction.' When the [National Recovery Administration] was declared unconstitutional in June, workers were overwhelmed by desolation. One Callaway worker wrote: 'We couldn't be in a worse fix than we are now.'[53]

***

The saddest part of this story is, of course, the unnecessary violence and death. For at least fifteen years, the Callaways had warned their employees that union activity in LaGrange would result in "violence, disorder -- and death!" But here's the curious thing about that warning: In all of my research, I haven't come across a single instance of violence perpetuated by the strikers or union members. All of the bloodshed seemed to come at the hands of those who represented the mill owners' interests. Perhaps the Callaways had to make sure that their promise of violence, disorder and death came true.

The *Spartanburg Herald-Journal* reported on March 4, 1935 that Manchester mill strike leader W.L. Stroup was "abducted from his home by several masked men, taken to a peach orchard several miles away, and beaten. He said he was told: 'We want to stop you from making speeches to mill workers.'"[54]

The violence toward union members continued even after the strike had ended. A memo from the Southern Labor Archives at Georgia State University reports that LaGrange union member Robert Henry was beaten to the verge of death on October 19, 1935.[55]

"I was on my way home and noticed a light blue Plymouth car," Henry said. "As I got close to it, I recognized Abner and Ben Knopp, who stepped out from behind the car. Then others raised up from the inside of it and I again was able to recognize one of the others who was in the car as Paul Garrison. They drew guns on me and told me to throw up my hands, but before I had a chance, they began to beat me over the head and face with the pistols they held and I was knocked down."

They put a sack over his head, threw him into the back of the car, drove into a deserted area outside of town, and beat him until he was forced to feign unconsciousness: "They were sure they had me more than knocked out this time. They would bend my fingers back as well as beat me on the leg again to see if there was any life left. After they pulled me out of the car, they placed me in a ditch on my face, then started beating on me again. I played off that I was knocked out. They then started up the car and left."

The car returned a few minutes later. Henry hid in the bushes, and he recognized the driver of the car as Tom J. Davis, an overseer at Dunson Mill.

Just three days before, Henry's friend Hugh Profit, an employee at Dunson Mill, had made the following statement: "This A.M about 9 o'clock I was told by Mr. Tom J. Davis that I had better stop going with Robert Henry and C. Davis, as I would get in trouble, and if I did not want some of it, that they were sure going to work on Robert Henry."

Two days after Robert Henry's beating, Hugh Profit "was telling Mr. T.J. Davis about Henry being beat up and which he then told me that I had better not talk or know too much, or else I would be the next one to get it. He also told me that Henry should have had his head cut off."

Four days after the beating, the following note was tossed into Henry's yard: "Robert Henry: After what happened the other night we would suggest that you leave LaGrange, and this is to notify you that you have thirty days from now to move yourself and family out of this town. It will be the best interests of LaGrange, yourself and family to heed this friendly warning, else we will have to do something that we do not want to do. - Citizens of LaGrange."

S.A. Hollihan, a representative of the Georgia Federation of Labor, tried to see that justice was served to the six men who kidnapped Robert Henry and "beat him up very unmercifully and threw him out of the car for dead." Hollihan said he had solid evidence to identify the men, and he hired an attorney. A Grand Jury was convened in November 1935. Hollihan reported on November 18, 1935: "The Grand Jury failed to return an indictment against the thugs identified by Robert Henry last week. We have secured a list of the Jury men and their connections, and it resembled more a stock holders meeting of textile manufacturers rather than a Grand Jury."

Hollihan had a hard time getting any press coverage of the case: "It just doesn't make news for the daily papers of Atlanta." But he didn't give up. He tried to get the Robert Henry case "before all government agencies possible." He turned over all of the evidence to the Federal Bureau of Investigation. The FBI investigator said there wasn't enough evidence to prosecute. According to the Southern Labor Archives memo, local mill workers believed that "the failure to prosecute was due to the desire of the Bureau not to offend Mr. Callaway."

Robert Henry and his family left LaGrange. He probably went to work for a WPA program. At least he got out alive. Fonie Stephens wasn't so lucky.

The *LaGrange Daily News* reported on May 13, 1935:

> Stephens, injured April 29 in a clash with troopers at the residence occupied by Charlie Moore, evicted striker, died in Dunson hospital late Saturday.
>
> Doctors issued a statement in which they said death was due to complications resulting from bruises about the head. The doctors added that a weak heart might have contributed to the death.
>
> The report filed at military headquarters said Stephens, one of more than a score of men who assembled at the house on Park Avenue early Monday morning two weeks ago, attacked a guardsman as he entered the house and that the latter retaliated with his fists. The report continued that a few minutes later when Stephens was being taken to a

truck to be transported to headquarters, he resisted again and another guardsman subdued him with his fists.

Adjutant-General Lindley Camp came to LaGrange at noon today to investigate into every detail of the clash and circumstances connected with the death of Stephens. He said that 'if any of the national guardsmen have overstepped their duty and authority they will be punished.'

The report to headquarters said further that Stephens did not appear to be badly hurt but that when others arrested were transported to Fort McPherson, he was left behind [at headquarters].

A few days later he was given additional medical treatment, after first aid had been rendered when he was first brought to headquarters. He was then permitted to go to his home, 612 Murphy Avenue. Complications followed and he was given hospital treatment.

Stephens was a World War veteran, 38 years of age, and had been employed with Callaway Mills eight years before he walked out on strike.

If Stephens was not badly hurt, then why wasn't he transported to the military internment camp at Fort McPherson with all of the other prisoners? Why was it "a few days later" before he received medical treatment beyond first aid? Also, weren't *all* of the national guardsmen overstepping their duties? Why were soldiers protecting Callaway's interests and helping to evict strikers from mill-owned housing in the first place?

Other people must have had questions about the official story, too. Two soldiers were charged with killing Fonie Stephens. The *LaGrange Daily News* reported on May 15, 1935:

Two Georgia national guards stood acquitted by a court martial here today on charges of killing Fonie M. Stephens, textile striker during eviction of strike families from Callaway Mill owned homes.

The verdict was handed to Major Herbert C. Hatcher of Waynesboro, trial judge advocate, a short time after the court began deliberation on the case. It said the soldiers, Sergeant Seaborn T. Stone and Corporal Orwell D. Smith, both of Atlanta, were shown by the evidence to have been attacked by the striker and retaliated with their fists in self defense . . .

The court martial received the case after hearing Dr. Enoch Callaway, acting medical advisor to the national guard, testify the bruises the striker received in his clash the with guardsmen were not in themselves sufficient to cause his death.

He testified the striker, Fonie Stephens, died of streptococcic cellulitis, a form of erysipelas [skin infection], but added that the bruises were a secondary cause. Dr. Callaway said Stephens had a 'markedly large heart' and at times poor heart action and that this also was a secondary cause of death . . .

Colonel L.C. Pope of Dublin, commanding officer of the guardsmen on duty here to prevent disorder in the strike, told of the guardsmen ordered to stand by while civil authorities proceeded with evictions of strikers from mill-owned homes to make room for other workers.

At the home of Charlie Moore, he said, two bailiffs were driven away when they tried to evict the family. Guardsmen were ordered to the scene and Captain Joseph Sauers of

Savannah, the colonel said, was struck by a man with a chair and seized by a woman. Meanwhile, Smith and Stone approached the porch.

As they took a hand in the conflict, Stephens stepped into trouble also, Colonel Pope said, grappling with Sergeant Smith. Sergeant Stone also grabbed the man and a fight resulted which ended as a third guardsman stepped into it and he and the civilian fell off the porch.

Colonel Pope said he called the physician to treat the men, who apparently were not badly hurt, though they had bruised eyes. He said Stephens had been detained and released 'subject to my call.' Stephens, he added, told him he had high blood pressure for years.

Mrs. Lucile Moore, sister-in-law of Stephens, also testified, weeping as she talked. She said the bailiffs started the fight and the troopers were standing on the porch at the time. Dr. Callaway, following her to the stand, said he found no injuries in his examination of Stephens except severe bruises, black eyes and a scratched face. Stephens was removed to a hospital after he began to develop a temperature at his home.

Since Dr. Callaway was the nephew of Fuller E. Callaway, Sr., why was he even allowed to testify, given his tremendous conflict of interest? If Dr. Callaway was correct – if Stephens died of a lethal skin infection – would Stephens have gotten the skin infection without the bruises from the soldiers? Would Stephens have died if he had received proper medical treatment quicker than "a few days" after the incident? Finally, after reading the above article, I have to wonder: Did Fonie Stephens die because he stepped into a fray to protect a hysterical woman from armed soldiers?

***

The violence, disorder, and death devastated the citizens of LaGrange. Historian James Lorence describes the aftermath of the strike: "The long-term implications of this result were profound: in the wake of the failed strike, many workers withdrew support for unionism and set the stage for future reluctance to embrace collectivism as the answer to worker problems. This growing resistance to labor organization, together with the historical amnesia concerning the militancy of 1934 [and 1935], was to seriously damage the interests of workers and discourage unionism, thereby contributing to a low-wage future for Georgia workers."[56] In 1937, a UTW representative reported that LaGrange workers were still "at the mercy of the Callaways."[57]

But was the strike really all for nothing? If nothing else, the strike proved that the lintheads of LaGrange had the guts to stand up to Callaway. It also proved that poor black and white people could work together against their oppressors, even in the South. Lorence describes the cooperation among the working class: "Although the mass organizations of the 1930s Georgia were eventually weakened by widespread adherence to Jim Crow social practices, the power of capital, the relative weakness of the union tradition, and the omnipresent specter of race, an examination of the unemployed movement and popular reaction to radical initiatives, especially among the African American jobless, demonstrates that a subtle collectivist theme was present in Depression Georgia."[58]

The fact that poor blacks and whites helped each other out during the depression seemed to scare the hell out of their feudal overlords. Lorence continues:

36

Alarmed by accounts of radical inroads among black and white workers, the press worked to link unionism with Communism. *The Atlanta Georgian*, for example, cited 'public evidence of Communism in Atlanta and in textile centers in the Carolinas,' while warning that the Communist Party was actively 'bending its efforts to bring about negro equality in the Southern textile mills' and injecting into the strike 'a racial issue that does not now exist' . . .

Indeed, the organizational activity of the Depression years actually raised the possibility of a breakthrough in interracial action, as the economic crisis failed to discriminate among the poor on the basis of race. Consequently, some of the protest demonstrations, marches, and other activities of unemployed organizations were carried out on an integrated basis. While the unemployed movement proved willing to explore such interracial cooperation, the challenge thus raised to traditional social practices opened it to criticism from the economic and social elite who controlled Georgia's political and social system in the 1930s . . . The advances of the Depression era were a testament to the power of economic hardship to open new fault lines in the structure of a southern society that was slow to modernize. Despite their modest scope, these halting steps marked a significant line of departure from the past . . .

While the mass jobless organizations of 1930s Georgia were eventually vanquished by adherence to Jim Crow, the heavy hand of state authority, the power of capital, and the specter of radicalism, the history of the state's unemployed movement demonstrates that worker organization was, at least for a time, embraced by the impoverished masses as a sensible response to economic adversity. And while the uneasy cross-racial coalition building of the 1930s slipped into memory, the civil rights movement was to witness another effort to build and alliance between black activists and white liberals on behalf of the liberation movement and legislative advances of the 1960s.[59]

Besides making important strides in cross-racial coalition building, the lintheads' strike led to greatly improved labor conditions. The Wagner Act (National Labor Relations Act) was passed in July 1935, just a few months after the strike in LaGrange. The Wagner Act outlined illegal employer practices such as restricting the right to collective bargaining, interfering with labor organization, and discriminating against employees.

Then, in 1938, the Fair Labor Standards Act outlawed the employment of children under the age of 16. Previously, young children were still commonly employed as "helpers" in the textile mills. This Act also established the minimum wage, the 40-hour work week, and overtime pay. It seems that we all owe a big "thank you" to the lintheads who resisted unfair labor practices. Yet few people alive today appreciate their legacy.

Frank Beacham, whose grandfather survived the "Bloody Thursday" massacre at Chiquola Mill in Honea Path, South Carolina, explains why history seemed to forget about the lintheads so quickly: "There was a campaign of fear and intimidation after the shootings that effectively erased public discussion of what had happened. Fearful workers who wanted to keep their jobs put a self-imposed lid on their own past. Somehow, as the years went by, the violence at Chiquola evolved into a source of shame. Many myths have built up over the years about the workers who died . . . They were called an isolated group of troublemakers and rabble-rousers. Some, mainly the mill's former management, claimed they deserved what happened to them. I see it another way. I think these mill workers risked everything -- their jobs, their freedom and ultimately their lives -- for a cause they believed in."[60]

Who are the heroes of this story? The Callaways? Or Fonie Stephens and all the other lintheads who tried to make FDR's words a reality?

***

In 1988, while working on a seminar paper, Mark Langford interviewed several LaGrange residents about their experiences during the 1935 strike. These interviews are now available at the Troup County Archives.[61] Most (if not all) of the people who were alive to remember the strike are now dead at the time of my writing. Langford's interviews give us a unique perspective: the perspective of the lintheads in LaGrange. Let's see what they had to say about the strike.

Mary Lewis worked in the spinning room at Unity Mill at time of strike, and her husband worked in the twister room. Mary had been working in cotton mills since she was 13. When she first started working in the mills, she worked 12 hours a day, 5 days a week, plus 6 hours on Saturday for a total of 66 hours a week.

Mary and her husband both went on strike in 1935, but like most who participated, she later developed an anti-union attitude: "I didn't know what it was like when we joined . . . And it caused, you know, hard feelings with a lot of people. And we didn't accomplish anything by it. To tell you the truth, I don't like [unions] . . . but I guess if it hadn't been for the union, the people never would've gotten any higher wages or anything like that if it hadn't been for a strike. But it looked like it could have been settled in a different way, doesn't it?"

Mary explained that the "stretch-out" was the main reason for the strike at Callaway Mills: "I was in spinning. And see, I think I was running eight sides, and they wanted to put us on 16. And that was just too much, you know. You just stayed in a mess all the time. You worked and you struggled. And we wasn't making nothing. I can't remember now what we was making. I think we worked a whole week for about eleven dollars."

After the strike got underway, "Governor Talmadge sent the National Guard in," Mary said. "Yeah, and he said he wouldn't do it . . . And they elected him and then he sent the National Guard in the next day."

Mary's husband, like many other men who participated in the strike, went to work for the Civilian Conservation Corps (CCC). As a part of FDR's New Deal, this public work relief program gave unemployed people some work and a little money. The CCC cleared off Pine Mountain (15 miles south of LaGrange), now the site of FDR State Park, and created the Pine Mountain Valley community.

"They put the men to work," said Mary. "They'd take 'em to Pine Mountain. They cleaned that place up down there . . . . They cleaned off Pine Mountain, you know, cleaned it off and everything. And then when we left we moved to Pine Mountain and we homesteaded . . . We had forty acres of land and a six-room house they built us . . . We had gardens and everything like that. We lived there five years and I think that was about the happiest life we ever had. It really was. We raised everything we had to eat, except our sugar and coffee. We raised our own wheat, our corn; we made our flour and meal; we raised our potatoes; we raised our meat. We had everything . . . We had four milking cows. We had all the milk and butter we wanted."

Mary's daughter Ruth Laney was only five years old at the time of the strike: "I remember the Guardsmen coming and being around the plant, around the mill, and my sister and I, we would go down to my grandmother's house on Dunson Avenue, and they would try to talk to us. And they would have big guns, and me being five years old, of course, it scared me to death. And I would take her hand, and we would run around the mill, around Dunson Avenue to my grandmother's house."

Still, Ruth followed in her parents' footsteps and went to work in the cotton mills. As a mill worker, even years later, she still felt the impact of the strike: "From that day forward, through the plants here in LaGrange, when Callaway -- Callaway had the plants at the time -- but you would get fired when I worked in the plant if anybody said anything about a union, or anything like that. You would have gotten fired. You was not allowed to -- you know -- anybody that talked about a union, they didn't value their jobs very much because they didn't have a job if the right person heard 'em, you know, because they was fired. Callaway Mills just did not allow unions to come into their plants. And Milliken, he has the plants now, and he doesn't either, which is, I think, a good thing, because Callaway, I think, was pretty good to the people. He provided a pool, a swimming pool for the families that worked for him and their children, and recreation, and we just have a lot of things here that Mr. Callaway did provide for us . . . After I got to be a teenager, we had clubs and everything that Callaway sponsored. We had a CEA that we could go to and play games and things like that . . . It didn't cost us a dime. He had dancing classes that he gave to the employees' children -- didn't cost us a dime. And, I think, from the time of the union, things got better for the people that worked in the plant."

"Old Man Callaway [Fuller Sr.] was real good to his employees," said Ruth's mother Mary.

At Christmas time, Ruth explained, "everyone in the family would get a bag of candy, all kinds of candy, then they'd get a bag of oranges and apples, and nuts, and they'd give 'em a ham and a turkey. And we'd draw a big bonus."

Like her mother, Ruth developed a strong anti-union attitude: "I think half the people that went out on strike really did not know what it involved. Most of 'em was uneducated, and they just took the union man's word. I think that's what it boils down to."

LaGrange resident Ora Woodham also remembered the strike. She didn't go on strike, but her husband did: "My husband was out on strike. He stayed out about four days, and he went to get groceries, and they wouldn't let us have 'em because he was on strike. We had to buy on credit then. So he said, 'Well, I'm going back and going to work.'

"So he started down the street, and a bunch of men was sitting out there and asked, 'Where you going, Bill?'

"He said, 'I'm going to work.'

"'Naw, naw," they said.

"'We don't have any groceries,' he said.

"They said, 'Well, you go uptown to the welfare, and they'll give you some groceries.'

"So he went up there, and they said, 'Yeah, we'll give you groceries but you've got to report for the WPA [Works Progress Administration, a New Deal work relief program similar to CCC] for 15 cents an hour Monday morning.

"And he said, 'Un-uh, I'll go back to work and make 30 cents an hour.'

"So he went back to work."

Ora explained that the "stretch-out" or Bedaux system was the main reason for the strike: "If you come up in the red, they got all over you, and if you come up short too much, they'd let you go."

Ora also recalls the experience of living under martial law in LaGrange: "We were not even allowed to turn our porch light on at night. We had to stay in the house. If we got out in the daytime, we had to be careful of what we said."

"When they started throwing people out of their houses over there on Park Avenue, then it was pretty hard. But I didn't go over there. A lot of people did, and watched it, and then they was really mad, you know, at the Guardsmen. And one man was killed. I don't know what happened, or the reason they killed him, but anyway, it was rough."

"It just tore up LaGrange and people we had known all our lives. At one time I knew everybody in this village. And when that happened, they moved out and brought others in. In fact, Callaway asked us in the mill -- everybody who had extra bedrooms -- to let these people that was coming to stay. We had a family from Comer, Georgia. And they were real nice, a man and his wife. Anyway, we just didn't know anybody after that, you know, except so many new people coming in. And still don't."

Ora was left with hard feelings about the strike: "I think [the strike] was a mistake because they really wasn't organized good enough 'cause they hadn't been organized very long."

Ora's husband Bill Woodham said that he felt like he was forced to join the union because of his career goal: "I was so poor I couldn't hardly afford to join the union. But I was trying to learn how to fix looms back at that time, trying to improve myself, improve my earning power, you know, and the loom fixers there in

Hillside Mill let me know right quick that I had to join the union if I expected any cooperation from them to learn to fix looms.

"I was weaving when the strike came off in 1935, and we got a notice from the plant that if we weren't back on the job by a certain date, they would consider us quit our jobs and place someone else on the jobs. I went back to the mill to get my job back on the last day, which was on Friday, and my overseer told me he didn't have room for me, that they had all the looms running and they didn't need me. And so I went back. I didn't know what in the world to do, but I run into Mr. Buck Prieston. Mr. Buck Prieston gave me a slip of paper with a number on it and told me to go down to the employment office and sign up and come back to work because they needed me. So I went down there and signed up, and they just took my name and sent me back to the mills to work. I went in, and there was my looms standing just like I had left them. They had never been touched. I learned then that in fact I didn't know who to believe -- the union or the mill's side.

"Now, the union people promised all kinds of things, which I found later were just false promises . . . They were promising better wages, better standards of living, such as that, and other things.

"When I got back [at the mill] I noticed that other people were coming in there that didn't even work there -- because they were on welfare working for the WPA, I believe they called it. They'd come in the same gate I did. I followed 'em through one morning. They went all the way through the plant. They had to go through the plant, around the plant, beside the plant, and then go out the other gate. I went in the back gate and they walked on through the front gate on to their jobs, WPA jobs. I found out that management was using that as a way of getting [artificial] numbers so that they could tell the media that the strike was just about broke when, you know, it wasn't. They would claim that had a certain percent of the people back at work . . ."

This reported fudging of numbers seems to be confirmed by a March 6, 1935 *Atlanta Georgian* article which states: "Fuller Callaway, Jr., treasurer of the mills, said yesterday that 80 percent of the number of employees were at work. Labor officials, however, said that 71 percent of the employees were on strike."

"We didn't know which way to turn," Bill continued. "And we suffered from it. The people here suffered from it. I know they had to move the people out of the houses that didn't come back to work. And they brought the National Guard troops in here to move 'em out."

Bill didn't recall any violence at the picket lines. The strikers "called us scabs" but "never did forcibly" prevent people from going into work, he said. Still, martial law was declared for the second time in six months, and Bill couldn't even speak to his neighbor on the street without being harassed by soldiers: "I had just been to the grocery store. I just lived about a block from the grocery store, just a few houses from the grocery store. I met a man that he and I was both working in the plant. We stopped and exchanged a few words. Well, here come two soldiers in a jeep and they told us to break it up, to get away from there. We wasn't allowed to stop and talk on the streets. Just two of us standing and talking to each other, neighbors, friends. We weren't even allowed to speak to each other on the streets."

Bill's brother was arrested by soldiers and placed in an internment camp: "I had a brother, just younger than me, that was arrested during one of the evictions . . . Robert Reed Woodham. They called him Red. He was red-headed. He was just standing there watching 'em. And I think he made a cursing remark about the soldiers throwing the stuff out of the house, and they arrested him and put him in a military camp."

Of course, memories cannot be trusted 100 percent, but Bill's memories suggest that there may have been another murder victim besides Fonie Stephens: "This man lived on Stonewall Street . . . and I had worked in the mill with his son. He was an elderly gentleman, and he tried his best to keep the soldiers from coming into his house, and they just run a bayonet through him. Killed him, of course. Now, there wasn't never nothing done about it . . . Seems like [his name] was Smith. They lived on the corner of Stonewall and Taft Street."

Bill certainly seemed to remember the details quite vividly. Fonie Stephens, if you recall, was killed on Park Avenue, and the soldiers who killed him were court-martialed. In my research, I have not seen anything else about a second murder on the corner of Stonewall Street and Taft Street. Perhaps, as Bill recalled, an old man was killed with a bayonet and there was simply never anything done about it.

When interviewing Bill, Mark Langford asked, "Did the legal officials here in LaGrange do anything, play any kind of role -- the police, sheriff's department, or mayor?"

"They were afraid to," said Bill. "They were afraid of Mr. Callaway."

Like his wife Ora, Bill was left with hard feelings about the strike: "It sure did hurt us financially. But it taught us a lesson. It taught us the lesson to be careful who you listened to, who you take advice from. That's one of the lessons I learned from the strike . . . Yes, I felt like the union betrayed me."

"I think [the failure of the union in 1935] is one of the reasons now that major industries here in LaGrange don't have unions," he said.

It seems like all of the Callaway Mills employees who went on strike felt betrayed by the union. The workers came together under the union banner to protest wage cuts and the Bedaux stretch-out system because it was going to eliminate hundreds if not thousands of jobs during the height of the Great Depression. The governor sent the state militia into town, arrested strike leaders, placed several people in military internment camps, and killed at least one man, thereby ending the strike. Still, somehow, the Callaways emerged as the heroes, great patriarchs and providers.

I am left wondering why virtually all of the anger felt by strike participants was directed at the unions instead of the Callaways. But I guess the working class heroes of LaGrange didn't have much of a choice, knowing that there was a good chance they'd have a rifle pointed at their temple or a bayonet shoved through their guts if they said otherwise.

Bill Woodham went so far as to say that the people of LaGrange would have starved to death if Fuller Junior wasn't there to provide for them: "[Cason Callaway] pulled out [of the cotton mills after the strike] and went to Callaway Gardens, formed Callaway Gardens down there in Harris County. In other words, he just got his money and retired. But Mr. Fuller Callaway Jr. stayed on and kept the mills running. If he hadn't, we'd all starved to death."

(Here I am reminded of Mary Lewis's statement that "the happiest life we ever had" was after they left the mills and moved to the Pine Mountain area to homestead and grow their own food. They didn't starve to death. They seemed to do just fine without a mill daddy.)

"[Callaway] is one of the smartest men I've ever known in my life," Bill Woodham continued. "I'm a great admirer of him . . . . He went far beyond other plants because he built things here for the good of the people. That's one thing I admire about Mr. Callaway. And he built equal things. When he built a swimming pool for the white people, he built one for the colored people and it was segregated. Whatever he did for the whites, he'd do for the blacks, and I admire him for that. "

Everybody loved that damn swimming pool, didn't they? It was perhaps the smartest investment Callaway ever made.

When examining the attitudes of LaGrange citizens toward the unions, we must also be cognizant of the fact that Callaway seemed to control the local press as well. When the first strikers walked out on February 28, 1935, the *LaGrange Daily News* ran a front-page story titled "Go back to your jobs!" and warned (just as it had in 1920) that Callaway just might take his golden eggs elsewhere if the strike continued:

> This community now faces the most serious moment in its entire existence. It has been brought about by the misunderstanding by the textiles workers of this community of the true situation facing all of us. We have only the greatest sympathy for every honest worker in our mills. There is no finer group of men and women in the textile mills of the United States than the great majority of those living here in LaGrange. The pity of it is that they have been misled by a radical few who have no stake or vital interest in our community.

> Their action jeopardizes the continuance of the mills of LaGrange. Our understanding is that the mills will continue to operate if there are workers who care to work and that

every legal protection will be given to the workers. The last resort of the mill management, we believe, will be the closing up and boarding up of the properties. Every worker in the mills who is worthy of the name of a citizen of the community -- every merchant and professional man in LaGrange entitled to call themselves by the name of a Lagrange citizen and every person who values his home, his church, his schools, and the other institutions the community built up through the years must join forces to end that LaGrange mills continue to operate.

Failing in that, LaGrange citizens had just as well fold up their tents, close up their places of business and seek their fortune elsewhere. The business men and the good workers and the professional men of this community are all tied up in one bundle and their economic existence depends completely on the continuance of the mills.

Callaway seemed to have great influence over the press and was adept at shaping public opinion. I wouldn't be surprised if the above article was actually written by a PR firm in Atlanta, just as the 1920 anti-union articles had been.

At the time of the Callaway Mills strike, Luther Morris, Sr., worked in the twister room at Unity Mill. He worked 10 hours a day, five days a week, for $10 a week. He joined the union "just for the same thing anybody else joined it for, to try to get better working conditions."

Luther felt as if he had been blacklisted after the strike: "The superintendent there at Unity, I don't say that he made a list, but I heard that he called over a certain number of us, said we'd never work for Callaway again, and we didn't."

49

During the strike, like most men, he participated in the New Deal work relief programs: "I worked in Pine Mountain Valley and worked all around Troup County, anything from working in the cotton fields to digging ditches.

"After the National Guard got down here and had taken over, I got out of town and stayed out . . . A bunch of men standing there with rifles on their shoulders and in their hands with bayonets stacked on 'em and us with nothing. How could we do anything? I didn't like it worth a cuss but there wasn't nothing I could do about it because they had guns and I didn't.

"I know they had one machine gun because I know where it was put up and mounted at. It was mounted right in front of the door of the office at Unity Cotton Mill . . . They had this machine gun sitting right in front of the dang door pointed just like I'm pointing, straight out to the street there. And it was ready to go."

Local law enforcement officials could not be trusted to protect the people, said Luther: "They went along with what he wanted to do . . . Callaway was boss here. When he said squat, they squatted . . . This was Callaway's town, mister, and don't you forget it. What he wanted to do, he done and got done."

Still, like everyone else who was interviewed by Mark Langford, Luther felt betrayed by the union: "I've got nothing to do for with a union. I felt they lied straight down the line. And they're lying today straight down the line. They aint nothing but a bunch of crooks."

Finally, Langford interviewed Jesse Maddox, who was personnel supervisor at Dunson Mill at the time of the strike. Maddox later became plant manager at the mill when it was bought out by Milliken.

Maddox may have been the only Callaway Mill employee who kept working through the 1934 general strike: "I worked right on during the 1934 strike. My bosses wanted me to write correspondence and everything and I was the only one who worked for the company, you know. The mill was shut down, but I still worked, you know, over at his house."

During the 1935 strike, Maddox was tasked with evicting strikers from their homes and hiring replacement workers: "After so long a time, we would give [strikers] a choice to either move out of the house or go to work. And so, then, we had to start, if they didn't move out of the house, we had to start proceedings to get a disposition warrant, and I had to have my young man to handle the disposition warrant. He had to give it to them, you know, before we could do anything about it and start forcibly moving them from the houses."

Maddox continued, "It got so rough that an appeal was made to the governor of the state to send the National Guard down, which he did, and I was for one very glad to see them. It was pretty bad. So I was very happy to see them come. I was hoping, you know, to get it straightened out. There was at least one person that was left dead. In the end he dies. It's amazing how he got killed. He was trying to obstruct one of the Guardsmen . . . The story was, the way I heard it was, the Guardsman, in more or less self-defense, hit at him with his rifle and happened to hit him in the head and knocked him down. I know there was one death that was reported. It was a wonder there hadn't been more because it was real vicious and the language that they used -- they called them everything but a white man. And this 'scab' business, that was just one of the real minor ones they'd call you and all. I was really happy to see the Guardsmen come in and, finally, as time went on, it began to ease up."

Maddox, as a close associate of the Callaways, seemed to take on the role of apologist during the interview. He said it was "amazing" how the murder victim was killed. He blames the victim, saying he "was trying to obstruct one of the Guardsmen." The Guardsman, on the other hand, was acting "in more or less self-defense" when he "just happened to hit him in the head" with his rifle. It's also interesting that Maddox says "there was one death that was reported." Perhaps he, like Bill Woodham, had heard of other unreported deaths.

"There are some things that happened that were really unfortunate," Maddox lamented. "There was things that happened that you wish hadn't happened. But, by large, I always thought that the mill down here was probably proved out of what the local companies have done for this area: the churches, foundations, the Callaway Foundation, and still a lot of educational schools and churches and things, My Lord, it's all over the place that they've done. All my children are alive now, but they came up on the influence with Callaway, and some of their spouses that come in here from other places, they couldn't believe the things down here that the Callaways built for people, like the CEA building, a swimming pool, a tennis place, the library, and all these things. The just can't believe it, you know."

Yes, it is unbelievable. When I tell friends from out of town that I grew up in a city that still had a "whites only" swimming pool and library in the 1990s, they just can't believe it, either. (By the way, shouldn't local governments be in charge of building swimming pools, recreation centers, and libraries for their citizens?)

At this time, I should point out that all of Mark Langford's interviews were conducted with white people. However, there were black men and women who worked for Callaway Mills in 1935.

They had the most unpleasant and lowest-paying jobs. They swept, scrubbed, cleaned bathrooms, opened bales, and performed other dirty jobs. Bill Woodham confirmed that black mill employees participated in the strike as well: "Yeah, they were too scared not to strike. They were working in the mills. Most of 'em were on WPA. We had very few blacks in the mills at that time . . . They were in segregated mill houses in 'nigger town' we called it."

CHAPTER THREE: PAPA COTTON'S HOMEGROWN RACISM & SEXISM

"Mr. Callaway told me that he didn't believe in segregation. He said he believed in slavery," reported Chris Boner, Director of the Callaway Educational Association (CEA) from 1979 through 1993, recalling his only personal meeting with Fuller E. Callaway, Jr.

My jaw dropped when I heard this as I interviewed Mr. Boner in April 2011.

Boner first came to LaGrange to serve as headmaster of LaGrange Academy, a private school that was founded as a reaction to the racial integration of schools in 1970. Because LaGrange Academy received a $150,000 grant from the Callaway Foundation, Mr. Boner kept hearing "more and more" about Mr. Callaway.

He decided to request a meeting with Mr. Callaway: "I finally just picked up the phone and called Mr. Callaway's office, talked to the secretary and told her who I was and what I had in mind, and she said, 'Well, he's here. Would you like to talk with him now?' I said I would. So I told him who I was and said I'd just like to meet you and come talk with you. Mr. Callaway was a wonderful individual to sit and talk with, but he had some extremely firm, fixed ideas about things. He asked me why we were getting tax exempt status [at LaGrange Academy]. To do that, you can't discriminate against race. '

"'If we don't get [tax exempt status],' I said, 'then the Foundation won't be able to give us that $150,000 we're asking for. Now, I'm not suggesting anything, Mr. Callaway, but if the Academy had a sugar daddy . . .'

"He looked at me and sort of grinned. He said, 'Boner' -- this is when he said to me -- 'I don't believe in segregation. People will tell you, I believe in slavery.' He said it in such a way -- I think he wanted to establish something between himself and me based on my stance on what he had just said. My immediate thought was that he wanted a reaction from me, but I wasn't going to give him one. And I didn't. I just let it go. I didn't say anything else . . . Then he brought me to the CEA, brought me to the library, and showed me around. It was a wonderful visit, but that particular comment just stuck with me."

Boner would eventually become the director of the CEA.

"At first I was director of Coleman Library, which was part of CEA, and then in 1979, when the director of the CEA retired, I was made director of the CEA," he said.

Boner also explained that although the discriminatory policies of the CEA were not written down anywhere, they were *de facto*: "It was *de facto* segregation, and it was soul-rending for me the whole time. [The CEA] was incorporated as a 501(c)(3) with membership requirements, and race was not one of the membership requirements. There was nothing in the articles of incorporation, nothing whatsoever, that a person could use to argue that this was an example of institutional racism *ipso facto* -- but anybody who lived around here knew that it was *de facto* racially segregated. But there was nothing in any kind of legal document that could be used to reject membership based on race.

"The other side is what actually happened . . . For membership in the CEA, you had to be proposed for membership by a member in good standing . . . CEA membership became more and more complicated for a couple of reasons. At one point, we actually had three black people who were members of the CEA. What happened was that a girl from LaGrange went to live in Jamaica for a long time, and she married a Jamaican man and had two children. They moved back to LaGrange, and she was a member of the CEA, so she came over to the CEA -- this is before I was the director, sometime in the 1970s -- to get a membership for her husband. At that time, if you wanted membership, you went to the library after a member proposed you. In this case, her husband didn't have to go to the library. She went to the library and proposed her husband for membership. So she went to the library and proposed her husband, and he became a member. And then they started bringing the kids over to play basketball in the children's basketball league.

"'Wait a minute, he can't be a member,' people said. 'He's a negro.'

"So, about the time I became director of the CEA, they made a lot of changes in the process to become a member. You still had to be proposed by a member in good standing, but you had to come to the CEA for an interview with the director of the CEA -- in other words, so somebody could lay eyes on you."

"Why weren't black people allowed to join?" I asked Mr. Boner. "Who made up the rules?"

"Nothing like that was ever talked about," he said.

I asked Mr. Boner if any black people had ever come to him for a membership interview when he was director of the CEA. He replied, "I had a lady tell me that she was going to bring her husband over for membership [in the 1980s]. In fact, they were people from my church at the time. I knew at the time she was married to a black man, and she was a member of a somewhat prominent family in LaGrange. Somebody came to me and said she was going to propose and that her husband was black. Somebody from the Foundation called me and said, 'She's married to a black guy, and she's going to try to get him membership.' I said, 'Well, what do we do?' Now, they didn't tell me not to accept him. They didn't say that. And this is crazy, but after I talked with my boss at the Foundation, I went to the membership book, and this lady's membership had been cancelled because she had checked out some books from Coleman Library and never brought them back, and if you didn't bring books back by a certain time, your membership could be cancelled. Her membership had been cancelled, so she couldn't propose. And when I called my boss at the Foundation, he told me to call the lady and tell her that she couldn't propose. I said, 'Well, why should I? I'm not going to call her.' He said, 'Well, what are you going to do?' I said, 'I'm not going to do anything.' And I never heard any more from her."

Boner told me that he never encountered any kind of protest against the institutional discrimination at the CEA, probably because the Foundation had also set up a counterpart to the CEA for black folks on the other side of town: "They also established on the other side of LaGrange the LaGrange Foundation for Negroes, which was the same thing as CEA. While I was at CEA, I was vice president of the board for the CEA and vice president of the board for LaGrange Foundation for Negroes [LFN], and I proposed that the LFN name be changed because it was just no longer acceptable. It never was acceptable in my mind. And so, I didn't think it would take much to vote and change the name -- but they couldn't because it was a legal corporation, so what they had to do was disincorporate and reincorporate as the Ogletree Street Educational Association, and they finally changed the name to William Griggs Recreation Center. Mr. Griggs was a black man who was principal of a school during integration and a supervisor and director over at LFN."

"On a personal level," Boner shared, "my wife would lose her patience with me because I was so torn about this idea. I was always torn by any kind of discrimination. The CEA was a heart-rending thing to me. At the same time, man, it did a heck of a lot of good stuff for a lot of people. And so did the Ogletree Street center.

"I don't quite know how to deal with my personal feelings about the CEA and my stay at the CEA. I wish I hadn't. I wish I had never gotten the job, because it was discriminatory and I didn't like that. By the way, it wasn't just racially discriminatory. It was discriminatory in other ways, but those other ways were much more subtle. The next most serious discrimination was against the poor, white people, while I was director of the CEA. They were the ones who were looked down upon. If you lived in Troup County [and if your skin wasn't too dark], you could become a member of the CEA, technically. We saw this type of discrimination at the pool a great deal. We also had discrimination against fat women. People would come to me in droves and even sign petitions to keep certain people away from the pool just because they were big, fat, ugly women . . . I hated the idea that an individual might be discriminated against. At the same time I was living with *de facto* discrimination in the organization."

To understand the scope and impact of the CEA, it's important to know that the organization was not a hole-in-the-wall social club with a few dozen or even a few hundred members. The CEA had approximately 10,000 members (and the population of LaGrange is approximately 28,000). It seemed like virtually all white people in LaGrange were members at some point (except for some of the poor, white people).

"How could this type of racial discrimination last until 1993?" I asked Boner. "Why did it last so long in LaGrange when similar practices had long since disappeared in other parts of the South? Was it because of the Callaways and their power?"

"To oversimplify, I would say yes, it was the Callaways," Boner replied.

"It was not too long after [Fuller E. Callaway, Jr.] died that these radical changes came about," he continued. "The CEA disincorporated and they gave everything to [LaGrange College]. The stadium went to the city and county. We gave the library collection to the public library."

***

After my interview with Mr. Boner, I decided to talk to some local black citizens about their feelings and thoughts on the CEA. This proved to be an extremely difficult task.

First I tried to set up a focus group to hear from several different citizens at once. I scheduled a meeting at the William Griggs Recreation Center. I recruited a friend who is active in local politics to serve as my co-moderator. We publicized the focus group through Facebook, email, and word of mouth, making sure to notify several leaders in the black community. Nobody showed up.

When we realized that nobody was going to show up, my friend invited me to accompany him to a coffee shop in a predominately black neighborhood. The coffee shop is owned by an older gentleman in his 70s or 80s who has been an anti-racism activist in

LaGrange for many years. The co-moderator told me that this gentleman would probably be happy to talk to me about his thoughts and feelings; further, he said, there would probably be other people at the coffee shop who could contribute to the conversation. As soon as we walked into the coffee shop, all eyes fell on me and my little notebook. As my friend explained my research to the owner, the few patrons who were in the coffee shop left. Not surprisingly (since our presence had caused his guests to leave), the owner seemed annoyed and said that he did not want to talk to me. I thanked him for his time. To be fair, the owner said I could call him and set up an appointment to talk to him at a later date. Now I realize that this would have been the most appropriate way to set up an interview, but my co-moderator thought that it would be okay to drop by the coffee shop unannounced, and I trusted his judgment. My co-moderator seemed a little embarrassed when his plan didn't work out. After we walked outside, he told me that a lot of black people in LaGrange, especially older people, simply don't trust white people.

After asking around and sending out more Facebook messages, I found a black gentleman who was willing to participate in an interview with me. He was in his 50s, a generation younger than the coffee shop owner. He told me about his experiences with racism when he was growing up, especially when LaGrange schools were integrated. That's when he first heard the word "nigger." He explained that the junior high schools were separated into boys' and girls' junior high schools after racial integration because white parents did not want their daughters in classrooms with pubescent black males.

However, when I tried to ask about the influence of the Callaway Foundation on local racism, his demeanor changed. He became shifty; his eyes darted around the room; and he seemed reluctant to say anything negative about the Foundation, even though he agreed that "Callaway had set up a system of separate but equal."

"I have friends in their 70s and 80s, and they have a different attitude about the Callaways," he said. "There's a different attitude from generation to generation. The first generation of black people to receive benefits from the Callaway Foundation appreciated it. Later generations had a more militant attitude toward the Callaways, and a lot of that is based on entitlement. It's all about people feeling that they're entitled to stuff."

This gentleman seemed to fall into the camp of those who appreciated the separate but equal facilities. He continued, "Before the Ogletree Street pool, people didn't know anything about how to swim. Because of that pool, today a lot of African Americans throughout the country and throughout the world, they can swim . . . I think that overall the Callaway Foundation was a benefit to this community."

I was dumbfounded by his position (and once again amazed by the public relations power behind swimming pools).

After the interview, I did some research and discovered that this gentleman was a member of an organization that has received millions of dollars from the Callaway Foundation over the years. He wasn't going to bite the hand that feeds him. And that's understandable.

Still, I hadn't been able to find a single black citizen who was willing to share his or her unfettered thoughts and feelings about the history of institutional racism in LaGrange. I decided to talk to someone from my own generation, someone whom I know personally, someone who might be a little more open and trusting. I contacted an old football teammate from my days at LaGrange High School. We met at a restaurant for a relaxed and informal interview. My friend shared his thoughts about growing up in LaGrange in the 1980s, at a time when there was still a "whites only" swimming pool in the city.

When he was a young child, his parents told him that the CEA swimming pool was "for rich people." And that made sense at the time because he knew "poor, white people went to the city pool" because that's where he went to swim, and he saw poor, white people there. But in fourth grade, he moved to a different school in a more affluent part of town (Hollis Hand Elementary School, named after Cason Callaway's wife Virginia Hollis Hand), and he learned that black people weren't allowed to swim in the CEA pool or visit the CEA library: "It wasn't in writing, but we knew. We knew we couldn't even walk on the grass there without getting charged with trespassing. Same with the library."

However, at the time, he didn't necessarily think of the segregation as being wrong: "We knew not to go there. It wasn't even an option, and we didn't know any other options." He didn't recognize the harmful effects of the segregation until he got older and looked back at his childhood.

I asked my friend how we might be able to help reduce racism and heal the community. He said, "By addressing the issue and not hiding from it."

That's what I'm trying to do with this book. Because race is still such a sensitive issue in LaGrange, I have had some concerns about publishing this book -- but I feel that this is a story that needs to be told. It's time to address the issue.

Some people have already expressed concerns about me "airing out the dirty laundry" of LaGrange, so to speak. I have tried to keep my book project under wraps for the most part, but I have told a few friends about it. One friend mentioned it to his roommate, who asked me about my research. After I briefly explained the premise of the book, he said, "You better watch what you write." I was at my friend's house at the time; his roommate and several of his roommate's friends were there, too. They were all white males. Within a couple of minutes, racist jokes began to fly in all directions. They weren't simply *racial* jokes about humorous cultural differences; they were *racist* jokes full of violence and hate. The crowd studied me, waiting for a reaction. I just walked away.

I have tried to approach this book project as a critical social science researcher. "The purpose of critical social science [CSS] research is not simply to study the social world but to change it," explains the author of *Social Research Methods*. "CSS researchers conduct research to critique and transform social relations by revealing the underlying sources of social relations and empowering people, especially less powerful people. More specifically, they uncover myths, reveal hidden truths, and help people to change the world for themselves."[62]

That is my aim: to reveal hidden truths and underlying sources of social relations, to help empower people with knowledge, and to help make our community a better place. Still, I wonder if a potential backlash from my work might exacerbate racial tension in the community. That is certainly a possibility. In the end, even if this book does lead to a few extreme reactions, I think that it's better for people know the truth. We are all living under the dark cloud of a secret, unspoken history that revolves around the Callaway textile empire, and I want to tell that story -- because I think that it will eventually help to empower people, even if it upsets a few at first. I think people should know that the Callaway swimming pool was originally built as a corporate tool to motivate young employees of Callaway Mills (who were not allowed to swim if they did not meet their work quotas); that black and white mill workers in LaGrange came together to fight for collective rights in a 1935 strike that ended with National Guard soldiers killing a man in front of his family; that other strike participants were beaten, arrested, and held prisoner in a military internment camp in Atlanta -- and that "newspapers in Nazi Germany crowed that this was a sign of fascism's coming global triumph"; that the Callaway Foundation seemed to have a vested, corporate interest in maintaining racial segregation in LaGrange; that we were and perhaps still are dangerously close to a fascist merger of government and corporate power; and that things don't have to remain *the way they are* simply because that's *the way they were*.

***

In addition to my interviews, I also conducted some basic quantitative research about the Foundation's influence on racist attitudes in LaGrange. I am not a research scientist, and my research was not approved by a university review board or published in a peer-reviewed journal (although I did receive feedback from my peers and professor in a graduate-level Research Methods course at the University of West Georgia). My research is incomplete and amateurish, but I think it's worth mentioning.

This was my research question: **Does former CEA membership predict current racist attitudes?**

In order to measure racist attitudes, I used a modified version of the 1990 Rochester Area Racial Attitude Survey developed by SNG Research along with University of Minnesota professors Dr. Michael Paige and Dr. John Taborn, and I created an online survey at kwiksurveys.com. The survey included several demographic questions as well as several items to measure racist attitudes. To limit the survey population to those who lived in LaGrange when the CEA was operational, I restricted participation to individuals who had lived in LaGrange for at least 30 years.

Participants were recruited through a letter to the editor of the *LaGrange Daily News*. The letter stated: "I am a psychology student at the University of West Georgia, and I am studying the development of racial attitudes in communities. I am writing to ask longtime LaGrange residents to help me with a class project by filling out a quick, easy, online survey. If you have lived in LaGrange for at least 30 years, please visit [the survey URL] and complete the survey. It contains 28 simple questions and takes about five minutes. Thank you very much for your help."

My letter was purposefully vague because the Callaway Foundation is still a powerful organization in LaGrange, and going into the specifics of the research may have prevented the publication of my letter to the editor.

The survey was completed by 28 participants. Remarkably, all participants were white, and only 19 percent of participants were *not* former members of the CEA. This suggests that the sample was not random. After all, many people do not read the newspaper, and many people do not have internet access.

It is interesting that only white people completed the survey. This may have been because the survey instrument itself was based on racial stereotypes and therefore inherently racist. For example, many survey items designated "White" as the default race and seemed to suggest that "White" is the race by which others should be compared. With this in mind, it is easy for me to imagine why a minority would not want to participate. In hindsight, I should have attempted to eliminate such bias from the survey questions. For example, instead of asking "Is it OK for whites to marry members of the follow groups?" I could have asked "Is it OK for people to marry outside of their race?"

Incidentally, due to limited time and resources, I decided to restrict my preliminary data analysis to the responses to this one particular item: "I think it is OK for whites to go on social dates with people in the following groups." The optional responses were: Strongly Agree, Agree, Neutral, Disagree, or Strongly Disagree.

The results suggest that former CEA membership may in fact predict current racist attitudes. Of the 28 participants, 67 percent of non-CEA-members either agreed or strongly agreed that it is OK for whites to marry blacks, but only 38 percent of former CEA members agreed or strongly agreed that it is OK for whites to marry blacks.

Despite the small sample size and other limitations, this simple survey may point to something. Participants who had been a member of the CEA were nearly twice as likely to respond, "No, it's not OK for whites to marry blacks." This is not surprising to me.

It's important to point out that correlation does not necessarily imply causation. In other words, CEA membership did not necessarily cause racism. People with pre-existing racist attitudes were probably more likely to join the CEA; thus, it could be that racist attitudes led to CEA membership. In reality, it was probably a little of both.

***

I don't blame Fuller E. Callaway, Jr. for being racist. Like me, he was a product of his environment. As a fellow son of LaGrange, I am racist, too. I think virtually everyone who grew up in LaGrange in the twentieth century is racist.

Don't get me wrong -- I don't want to be racist. I try to avoid it. But I must admit my racist tendencies in order to oppose them. We can't always control our unconscious reactions or what pops into our minds, but we can control how we react to it. We can ask ourselves, "Where did that thought come from? Why do I feel that way?"

According to the Harvard Implicit Association Test (IAT), I have a moderate automatic preference for European American compared to African American. The online test showed that it was easier for me to associate the concept of *bad* with black faces and *good* with white faces. Only 12 percent of participants who have taken the test at this time found it easier to associate *good* with black faces.

I encourage you to try the test for yourself at http://implicit.harvard.edu.

Malcolm Gladwell, a journalist who is half black, also took the IAT several times and discovered that he too has a moderate automatic preference for European American.

"So what does this mean?" asked Gladwell in his book *Blink*, which explores the power of split-second, snap judgments. "Does this mean I'm a racist, a self-hating black person? Not exactly. What it means is that our attitudes toward things like race or gender operate on two levels. First of all, we have our conscious attitudes. This is what we choose to believe. These are our stated values, which we use to direct our behavior deliberately . . . But the IAT measures something else. It measures our second level of attitude, our racial attitude on the unconscious level -- the immediate, automatic associations that tumble out before we've even had time to think. We don't deliberately choose our unconscious attitudes . . . . We may not even be aware of them. The giant computer that is our unconscious silently crunches all the data it can from the experiences we've had, the people we've met, the lessons we've learned, the books we've read, the movies we've seen, and so on, and it forms an opinion. That's what is coming out in the IAT."

"The disturbing thing about the test," Gladwell continues, "is that it shows that our unconscious attitudes may be utterly incompatible with our stated conscious values. As it turns out, for example, of the fifty thousand African Americans who have taken the Race IAT so far, about half of them, like me, have stronger associations with whites than with blacks. How could we not? We live in North America, where we are surrounded every day by cultural messages linking white with good."[63]

Imagine growing up as black child in LaGrange in the 1980s, knowing that you cannot check out books from the largest library or swim in the nicest swimming pool because your skin is too dark. Imagine what havoc that must wreak on the unconscious mind!

In her 1949 memoir *Killers of the Dream*, Lillian Smith described "the dance that crippled the human spirit" in the segregated South: "From the time little southern children take their first step they learn their ritual, for Southern Tradition leads them through its intricate movements. And some, if their faces are dark, learn to bend, hat in hand; and some, if their faces are white, learn to hold their heads up high. Some step off the sidewalk while others pass by in arrogance. Bending, shoving, genuflecting, ignoring, stepping off, demanding, giving in, avoiding. . . . So we learned the dance that cripples the human spirit, step by step by step, we who were white and we who were colored, day by day, hour by hour, year by year until the movements were reflexes and made for the rest of our lives without thinking."[64]

How can we move beyond the enduring power of our unconscious prejudices? It's not easy. As I mentioned before, one method might be to simply monitor your thoughts. When you notice a prejudicial thought, ask yourself, "Why do I feel this way? What is the source of this thought?"

Of course, this still constitutes a conscious mode of thinking -- but we may be able to influence the unconscious mind by changing our environment. For example, Gladwell found that people who read a story about Martin Luther King, Jr., before taking the IAT exhibited less implicit prejudice against African Americans.

Therefore, we may be able to reduce our unconscious prejudices by taking a chance, stepping outside our comfort zone, opening our minds and hearts, and making new friends. But first we have to stop pretending that we live in a color-blind society where racism is no longer a problem.

Michelle Alexander, author of *The New Jim Crow*, says, "Today in the so-called era of color-blindness, something akin to a racial caste system exists in America . . . It is a truth that we as a nation have gone to great lengths to deny, or perhaps it's more accurate to say, to avoid knowing . . . All institutions in our society are infected with conscious and unconscious bias."[65]

The problem, Alexander argues, is the "indifference to the suffering of people of other races" and the failure to see different races as fully human. It is a problem of dehumanization. She says that the civil rights movement of the 1960s was left unfinished: "What is needed today is a broad-based social movement . . . multi-racial, multi-ethnic that includes poor whites, a group that is often pitted against people of color, triggering the rise of successive new systems of control. But before such a movement can get started, a great awakening is required. We've got to awaken from this color-blind slumber we're in; [we've got to awaken] to the realities of race in America."

After the unprecedented cross-racial coalition building among mill workers during the strike of 1934-35, Callaway injected a lethal dose of racism into our community that would carry widespread segregation into the 1990s.

Five years later, in 1940, Callaway was lynched by an angry mob. Of course, I'm not referring to Cason, Fuller Junior, or any members of *the* Callaway family. I'm referring to Austin Callaway, a 16-year-old black child who had been accused of attempting to attack a white woman. *The Crisis* reported, "The lynching of 16-year-old Austin Callaway in LaGrange, Georgia, September 8 by a mob of six masked white men who forced the local jailer to release the boy from a cell, and then took him eight miles from town where he was shot to death, constitutes the sixth authenticated lynching of 1940."[66]

***

My mother died of cancer when I was 23. During her last few weeks, her mind often seemed to be somewhere else. She was fading. But when she was present (for moments at a time), she was fully present to me and for me, and she often offered the simple wisdom of a Buddha.

"Just be a good person, like your daddy. That's all that matters," she told me.

That was the last coherent thing she said to me. She said something else in those last few weeks that sticks out in my mind: *"I wish I had done something more with my life."*

That memory stings because I can remember criticizing her for "not having a real job."

"You're just a secretary!" I yelled during an argument (probably on more than one occasion).

I couldn't have been more wrong. She was a mother, and that is the most important job on Earth. But, on some level, I suppose I saw her as less valuable human being because of her job title and gender. Men should make more money than women, even at the same jobs, right? That's how it was in the 1980s, when I was growing up. And to a large extent, that's still how it is today. But things are getting better. We can look to the past to see how the situation has improved.

When Fuller E. Callaway married Ida Cason Callaway, "he initially gave her a household allowance of $6.25 a week. At the end of the first week, however, Callaway's new bride tearfully confessed that in setting up her new household she had spent an additional dollar. Callaway allowed his wife to 'borrow' the extra dollar she needed and then to repay the loan in ten cent installments over the next two and a half months. In the future, he told her, whenever expenses exceeded the allotted amount, the deficit would be subtracted from future allowances in small installments . . . As the family grew in size with the addition of children and relatives, Callaway increased the allowance, but Mrs. Callaway stayed within the limits of her budget."[67]

Mrs. Callaway once told her son Fuller Junior that as long as his father was bringing in the money, it was her duty to see that everything in the home ran to his satisfaction.

"Of course, at the turn of the twentieth century, such an attitude was accepted as the standard of wifely duty and responsibility," Whitley wrote in her Ph.D. dissertation on Callaway, "but it is fair to say that in the Callaways' case the partnership went further than normally might have been expected."[68]

Callaway's patriarchal system was based on a clear power hierarchy that separated humans into inferior and superior groups.

Gloria Steinem once said, "Sex and race, because they are easy and visible differences, have been the primary ways of organizing human beings into superior and inferior groups and into the cheap labor on which this system still depends."[69]

And in the South, the ties between sexism and racism may be even stronger. Journalist Gabriel Winant explains, "Racism has long kept white Southerners from forming the biracial alliance that progressives see as so obviously beneficial; but if racism is costly in this sense, in another it is a lucrative investment, and not casually abandoned. Gender norms keep the peace too. Southern white men have long understood that they are, as one historian has put it, 'masters of small worlds,' and a threat to one master is a threat to all."[70]

In the mill village of LaGrange, gender and race determined labor options. White women were allowed to operate some textile machinery in the mills, but they weren't paid as much as white men who worked the same machinery. The dirty jobs in the mills were reserved for black employees, and the dirtiest, lowest-paying jobs were reserved for black women. Ironically, though, many black women in LaGrange were trusted to work in the homes of prominent white families, cook their meals, and raise their children. One of the most striking features of the Callaway mansion (Hills and Dales Estate) is that every room conveys a sense of European royalty -- except for the stark, drab kitchen. That's where the servants worked.

Many of the same ways of thinking that perpetuate racism also perpetuate sexism. An authoritarian family structure, for example, teaches children that men are at the top of the hierarchy, followed by women, followed by children; mothers are subservient to fathers. In such a household, children come to see certain people as more powerful, more important, or maybe even more fully human than others who are lower on the hierarchy. The opposite of an authoritarian structure is an egalitarian family structure in which the mother and father act as equal partners.

Cultural critic Don Baker explains, "In an egalitarian household, children learn to make up their own minds because they see the parents have a dialog, and no one parent is always right. So they have to learn to determine right and wrong for themselves. But in an authoritarian household, all they have to do is obey, so they don't learn this. They tend to learn that 'might makes right' -- that the big guy makes the decisions, and whatever he says goes."[71]

Religious fundamentalism in the Bible belt also reinforces the patriarchal, authoritarian family structure. Those who interpret the Bible literally have plenty of ammunition for keeping "their" women submissive. Here are just a few examples:

"I would have you know that the head of every man is Christ, and the head of the woman is the man, and the head of Christ is God." - 1 Corinthians 11:3

"Women should remain silent in the churches. They are not allowed to speak, but must be in submission, as the Law says." - 1 Corinthians 14:34

"Wives, submit to your husbands as to the Lord. For the husband is the head of the wife as Christ is the head of the Church." - Ephesians 5:22-23

"Wives, submit to your husbands, as is fitting in the Lord." - Colossians 3:18

In LaGrange, throughout most of the twentieth century, Callaway-funded segregation kept the races divided (while maintaining the pretense of benevolent paternalism), and Callaway-funded churches kept women in their place (under men). Papa Cotton was in high cotton as the master of His small world.

CHAPTER FOUR: RELIGIOUS FUNDAMENTALISM

"Eleven o'clock on Sunday morning is the most segregated hour in Christian America." - Rev. Martin Luther King, Jr.

In LaGrange, there are plenty of fundamentalist churches where preachers teach that their interpretation of the Bible is the inerrant word of God. As a result, many fundamentalist churchgoers believe that there's only one right way to live -- their way -- and everybody else is literally going to Hell.

The 2011 sci-fi movie *Priest* offers a nightmarish glimpse of a future society ruled by religious fundamentalism. In the film, billboards towering above working-class drones display the words "Faith, Work, Security" as a disembodied voice repeats the mantra: "The Church will protect you. The City will protect you."

The scene is a chillingly accurate portrayal of fundamentalism, which thrives on fear and demands obedience. Thus, when Callaway felt threatened by the unions in 1920, local preachers earned their company paychecks by instilling fear and obedience in their congregations. Unity Baptist Church pastor W.P. Cofield went to work, telling his congregation: "The Law of Christ will cause the employed to respect their obligation to the employer and the community . . . Let us as the industrial people of the community, apply the law and principles of Jesus Christ in the mills by giving faithful, honest service, and in the community by living clean, wholesome, Christian lives."

Is it a coincidence that Samuel Slater, the Father of the American Factory System was also the Father of the Sunday School System? I don't think so! Throughout history, members of the ruling class have used religion to oppress and control the working class. Following Slater's example, Fuller E. Callaway invested heavily in local churches. Preachers were added to the company payroll. Callaway paid half of their salaries, and the other half came from their congregations.[72]

Fuller Junior continued his father's tradition. He set up special bank accounts for local ministers and told them, "Let me know when you need more money!"[73]

The tradition continues today through the Callaway Foundation. Charles Hudson, who married Fuller Junior's daughter Ida in 1955, explained in a 2003 interview: "The Callaway Foundation decided to help with all the churches in the City of LaGrange and we would fund fifty percent of any programs of building a church or parking lot for the church or a parsonage and that program lasted for a long time. I think the program has changed now, to where I think it's twenty percent now and it is for all the churches in LaGrange and Troup County. We also would help, back in the olden days, with churches in the county in the amount of ten percent of the amount they raised and fifty percent on the local churches. There was a number of years where a lot of money was spent on building churches."[74]

Why has this corporate outfit invested millions of dollars in building local churches over the years? Religious fundamentalism breeds obedience and submission -- not only in the church, but also in the workplace and community. It keeps people in their place on the hierarchy and maintains the status quo, which seems to be a primary goal for the people at the top of the hierarchy.

Unfortunately, fundamentalism also foments prejudice and violence.[75] Fundamentalism revolves around fear rather than love. For many Christian fundamentalists, Satan lurks around every corner, tempting humanity with the fruit of knowledge. Like Eve, women are weak and foolish; we are all fallen creatures, born into sin; and we should fear and distrust those who do not subscribe to the same close-minded belief system.

After the terrorist attacks of 9/11, Dr. James W. Jones, an Episcopal priest, clinical psychologist, and Rutgers University professor, set out to answer the following question: *Why does religion turn violent?* In his psychoanalytic exploration of religious terrorism, Jones discovered that fundamentalism perpetuates shame and humiliation: "I would suggest the more a religion exalts its ideal, or portrays the divine as an overpowering presence and emphasizes the gulf between finite human beings and that ideal so that we must feel like 'worms, not human' (in the words of the Psalms), the more it contributes to and reinforces experiences of shame and humiliation."[76] Further, Jones adds, there are "numerous studies correlating conditions of shame and humiliation with increases in violence and crime, especially for males."[77]

According to Jones, religious fundamentalism not only encourages violence by continually reinforcing shame and humiliation, but it also provides "socially approved" ways of releasing the violence: "By fomenting crusades, dehumanizing outsiders, and encouraging prejudices, fanatical religions provide ready, religiously sanctioned targets for any increase in aggression."[78]

Followers of fundamentalism cannot live up to their own ideals, Jones explains; they live in constant state of fear and shame, and they often take their frustration out on others: "Weighed down by this sense of badness, a person may identify with an idealized tradition or group and then project the sense of badness onto some outside person or group, thereby seeing some other group, race, or religion as evil. The experience of badness that the individual has taken into himself is so painful that often it must be discharged by being projected onto a despised group. Religious groups that encourage this splitting of the world into all-good and all-bad camps often find others to demonize and carry this sense of badness. Research on religious fanaticism and terrorism provides countless examples of this dynamic. It is not coincidence that this research has found the more fanatical groups are also the most racist, homophobic, and anti-Semitic . . . Such a denigration of the other, an almost inevitable result of the moral defense with its over-idealization of an object and the splitting of the world, makes the denigrated other a ready victim of terrorist violence."[79]

And so, in Mohamed Atta's letter to the terrorists who carried out the attacks of 9/11, he promised that their souls would be purified if they obeyed their orders and killed the enemy in one final, ultimate sacrifice.[80] Obedience. Submission. Purification. Earning divine favor. Jones argues that these are the central themes of patriarchal, fundamentalist religions.

"From a clinical standpoint," Jones concludes, "what appears most salient in the turn toward violence on the part of religion are the themes of shame and humiliation, the apocalyptic splitting of the world into all-good/all-evil camps, the wrathful, judgmental image of God, the drive for purification, and the authoritarian concern with submission and prejudice against outsiders."[81]

Here in LaGrange, fundamentalist churches have received Callaway corporate funding for generations. As a result, LaGrange is a hotspot for the apocalyptic splitting of the world that Jones describes.

Each year since 1997, thousands of fundamentalist followers flock to Faith Baptist Church in LaGrange and fork over $10 to experience the Judgment Journey, a theatrical vision of the apocalypse. For the past few years, the spectacle has attracted approximately 20,000 patrons each year. Visitors travel down a wooded trail to witness live-action scenes including the four horsemen of the apocalypse, the killing of martyrs, and the judgment of those who reject Jesus Christ. Of course, those who reject Jesus burn in Hell for all eternity, and this is graphically illustrated with a pyrotechnic show. A promotional video on YouTube.com includes the following quote from the *Columbus Ledger-Enquirer* newspaper: "Faith Baptist wants to scare the Hell out of you. Literally!"[82]

Each October, similar so-called "judgment houses" pop up in other hotspots of fundamentalism across the Bible belt. Many people seem to think of them as harmless haunted houses with bonus lessons in morality. But there's a big difference between a haunted house and a judgment house. When children emerge from a haunted house, scared and crying, their parents tell them it's not real; the monsters are only make-believe. However, when children experience the judgment journey, a preacher tells them that the end of the world is upon us, that Hell is real, and that they'll surely end up in Hell unless they obey.

This is nothing short of emotional child abuse. Think about it: If a parent were to threaten a child with a similar terroristic threat ("I'm going to lock you in the basement and burn your flesh if you don't obey!"), then the parent would be charged with a crime -- and for good reason: this type of emotional abuse often leads to permanent psychological damage. However, such threats appear to be socially acceptable when made by a fundamentalist church.

As an apocalyptic vision, LaGrange's Judgment Journey celebrates violence, disorder, death, and the end of our world. Jones explains, "Violently apocalyptic movements not only split the world into irreconcilable opposites of good and evil, they also look forward to the climatic end of history, when evil will be violently eradicated. Apocalyptic religion is not only about dividing the world, it is also about purifying the world. In the apocalyptic mind-set, purification is almost always bloody. Rather than envisioning a spiritual process through which the unholy is transformed into something holy, apocalyptic religions are full of fantasies and images of violence, warfare, and bloodshed in which the unholy is destroyed in the most gruesome fashion imaginable. Here purification becomes linked with violent death."[83]

In splitting the world into good and evil, judgment houses also promote the dehumanization of others. I've never been a patron of the Judgment Journey at Faith Baptist Church, but several years ago, out of curiosity, I visited its predecessor: the Hell House on Hamilton Road in LaGrange. In the first room of the Hell House, we saw a grieving mother overlooking a casket. Our group's demonic tour guide in the Hell House -- the only African American actor in the production -- informed us that the young man in the casket had been killed by God because he was gay. In another scene, a white teenager shot himself in the head with a handgun after listening to rap music. (Excuse my vernacular expression, but I was like, "WTF!?")

Fortunately, not all Christians believe in a judgmental, wrathful God. Even within the same church, people often have different ideas about the nature of God. In fact, one might argue that every Christian has his or her own image of God. Some believe in an angry god; others believe in a loving, forgiving god; others may believe in a new-age, non-anthropomorphized god that encompasses all energy in the universe; and some Christian churchgoers don't believe in a God at all. Jones points out that "punitive and wrathful images of God are associated with external locus of control, anxiety and depression, and less mature object relations. The reverse has also been found to be true, that a more benevolent internal representation of God is associated with more mature psychological development and the capacity for more mature object relations."[84]

In *The Fundamentalist Mind*, Stephen Larsen explores the neurobiology of fundamentalism and explains how, over time, the fundamentalist brain can become "hardwired" to see the world in black-and-white, good-and-evil terms. Despite this fact, Larsen reaches a hopeful conclusion: "Underneath the flawed neurology and psychology, the bad ideas, and the egregious theology, I believe a kind of natural religion awaits humanity. As we have seen, the capacity to respond to the splendor of the universe and the sacredness of life is built into our nervous systems. It seems clear that the healthier the nervous system, the more open the mind. And the more open the mind, the healthier the religion."[85]

How might people open their minds and break free from the shackles of fundamentalist thought? Several lines of recent research suggest that people do in fact have the ability to make their nervous systems healthier. In *How God Changes Your Brain*

(2010), Andrew Newberg and Mark Robert Waldman explore the neuroscience of spiritual practices such as meditation and contemplative prayer. Much recent research has focused on the anterior cingulate, which the authors describe as our "neurological heart." The anterior cingulate sits between the frontal lobe and the limbic system, where it integrates our thoughts and feelings. The authors explain, "If you have a large or more active anterior cingulate, you may experience greater empathy, and you'll be far less likely to react with anger or fear."[86] Numerous brain scan studies show that this area of the brain is stimulated by spiritual practices. Such stimulation offers many benefits: "The anterior cingulate plays a major role in lowering anxiety and irritability, and also enhance social awareness, a feature that tends to deteriorate with age."[87] A 2007 Emory University study found that Zen meditation provided "neuroprotective effects and reduced the cognitive decline associated with normal aging."[88]

Notably, the authors of *How God Changes Your Brain* found that people don't have to believe in God in order to experience the neurological benefits of spiritual practices: "We discovered that you could take God out of the ritual and still influence the brain. This is what our memory research demonstrated. Our patients were taught traditional Eastern meditation, using sounds and movements that had deep religious meaning, but we did not emphasize the spiritual dimensions of the ritual. No one reported having a spiritual experience, and no one even mentioned God."[89]

Spiritual practices such as meditation allow practitioners to lose themselves (their egos) in the reality of the present moment. Although people often associate spirituality with ideas about afterlives and past lives, neuroscience suggests that the primary benefit of spiritual practice is to help us connect (or reconnect) to reality in the present moment. Indeed, Newberg and Waldman conclude, "This evidence confirmed our hypothesis that prayer and meditation may have less to do with a specific theology than the ritual techniques of breathing, staying relaxed, and focusing one's attention upon a concept that evokes comfort, compassion, or a spiritual sense of peace."[90] Spiritual growth, then, does not seem to be bound to a specific religion or concept of God; rather, it seems to be predicated on transcendence of the ego by living wholly in the present moment.

Newberg and Waldman also explain how religious fundamentalism actually blocks spiritual growth: "The personality you assign to God has distinct neural patterns that correlate with your own emotional styles of behavior. For example, according to [a Baylor University] study, most of those who embrace an authoritarian god tend to favor the death penalty, want to spend more money on the military, want to give the government more power to fight terrorism, and insist that prayer should be allowed in public schools."[91] In other words, an authoritarian image of God leads to the problematic "Us vs. Them" mentality.

Whereas meditation activates the anterior cingulate (our "neurological heart"), anger shuts it down. "Anger is the problem," explain Newberg and Waldman. "And when anger is married to a specific ideology and organized into an institution -- be it religious or political -- then there is a real danger that individual hostilities will feed upon each other until an emotional tipping point is reached. At that moment, destructive irrational behaviors can more easily be expressed in the world. This is the underlying neurological basis for violence, and it all begins with the primitive fundamentalist traits that exist within the limbic brain."[92]

The best way to reduce such fundamentalist thinking, the authors conclude, is through education and exposure to other ideas. Teaching a fundamentalist how to meditate or practice contemplative prayer, for example, would likely be a rewarding exercise for all parties involved.

* * *

Throughout Western history, at least since the time of Ancient Greece, humanism has stood as the opposing force to fundamentalism. Humanism revolves around love rather than fear. In the eyes of humanists, we are not fallen creatures; we are a manifestation of the divine, and life itself is sacred. We may fall (and we may fall often), but we can choose to stand up. Instead of splitting the world into "Us vs. Them," humanists focus on the commonalities among all humans. We all suffer, for example, and Buddhists teach that this common ground should be the basis for compassion toward all humans.

Although humanism is typically associated with secularism, humanists may be either secular or religious. Around the world, more people seem to be opening their minds to the idea that maybe their culture's particular holy book is not the inerrant word God after all. *Maybe there is more than one way to live a good life.*

Protestant churches in Europe represent the cutting edge of religious humanism. Reverend Klaas Hendrikse of the Exodus Church in Holland says, "God is not a being at all. It's a word for experience, or human experience. When it happens, it happens down to earth, between you and me, between people."[93]

Instead of interpreting the Bible as the inerrant word of God, Rev. Hendrikse views it as a collection of mythological stories that offer wisdom about how to lead a good life.

Chris Hedges, Harvard seminary scholar and author of *American Fascists: The Christian Right and the War on America*, also promotes a non-literal interpretation of the Bible: "Genesis was not written to explain the process of creation, of which these writers knew nothing. It was written to help explain the purpose of creation. It was written to help us grasp a spiritual truth, not a scientific or historical fact."[94]

As more people embrace non-literal interpretations of ancient holy books, we may see an unprecedented integration of spirituality and science in the future. Religion may become more of a *practice* than a *belief*. On the other hand, a fundamentalist backlash could lead to an explosion of right-wing authoritarianism and drag humanity down into another Dark Age. (I sure am glad I'm an optimist!)

Without Callaway's funding of religious fundamentalism, we would still have fundamentalist churches in LaGrange, but probably not nearly as many -- and we would still have to deal with the harmful effects of prejudice and violence, but maybe not quite as much.

CHAPTER FIVE: RIGHT-WING AUTHORITARIANISM & SOCIAL DOMINANCE

"Resist much, obey little. Once unquestioning obedience, once fully enslaved." - Walt Whitman

Right-wing authoritarianism is a measurable personality construct developed by psychologist Bob Altemeyer. He spent most of his career studying authoritarianism because he sees it as "the greatest threat to American democracy."

Research shows that "people who have strong beliefs in religious fundamentalism are also likely to score high in right-wing authoritarianism."[95] Further, right-wing authoritarianism and religious fundamentalism predict prejudice against minorities.[76]

"Authoritarianism is something authoritarian followers and authoritarian leaders cook up between themselves," Altemeyer explains in his book *The Authoritarians*. "It happens when the followers submit too much to the leaders, trust them too much, and give them too much leeway to do whatever they want -- which is often something undemocratic, tyrannical and brutal."[96]

Before we delve into Altemeyer's work, allow me to explain the difference between *authoritative* and *authoritarian*. To be a successful parent, for instance, one must be authoritative; this involves establishing clear rules and clear consequences for breaking the rules. However, the authoritative parent also gives her children enough space to make their own decisions within the framework of the rules. The authoritarian parent, on the other hand, says, "My way or the highway!" and "Might makes right!" Under authoritarian parents, children learn how to submit to power, not how to think for themselves. It is this extreme type of submission, typically learned in the home at a young age, which drives authoritarianism.

According to Altemeyer, authoritarian personalities share three defining traits:

> 1) A high degree of submission to the established, legitimate authorities in their society;
>
> 2) High levels of aggression in the name of their authorities; and
>
> 3) A high level of conventionalism.[97]

"Because the submission occurs to traditional authority, I call these followers right-wing authoritarians," writes Altemeyer. "I'm using the word 'right' in one of its earliest meanings, for in Old English 'riht' (pronounced 'writ') as an adjective meant lawful, proper, correct, doing what the authorities said."

"Right-wing" then, in this sense, does not refer to the right wing of the political spectrum. There may be right-wing authoritarians (RWAs) on the left wing of the political spectrum. Communists in the USSR, for example, were typically RWAs who supported a left-wing political ideology.

RWA is a personality construct, not a political description. Altemeyer explains, "Right-wing authoritarianism is a personality trait, like being characteristically bashful or happy or grump or dopey."

RWA can be measured and quantified using the RWA scale developed by Altemeyer. Using a scale of +4 (very strongly agree) to -4 (very strongly disagree), test takers indicate the degree to which they agree or disagree with 22 different statements. I won't list all 22 statements, but here are a few examples:

"Women should have to promise to obey their husbands when they get married."

"Gays and lesbians are just as healthy and moral as everybody else."

"It is always better to trust the judgment of the proper authorities in government and religion than to listen to the noisy rabble-rousers in our society who are trying to create doubt in people's minds."

"Our country desperately needs a mighty leader who will do what has to be done to destroy the radical new ways and sinfulness that are ruining us."

At this point, you have probably noticed that RWA sounds a lot like religious fundamentalism. Indeed, researchers have often found it challenging to tease apart the relative influences of RWA and fundamentalism because there's so much overlap between these two constructs.[98] The fundamentalist worldview and authoritarian worldview often go hand in hand, reinforcing each other. Like fundamentalists, authoritarians tend to believe that the world is a dangerous place full of evil people.

"Since authoritarianism can produce fundamentalism if one grows up submissively in a religiously conservative family, and (conversely), fundamentalism can promote authoritarianism with its emphases on submission to religious authority, dislike of out-groups, sticking to the straight and narrow, and so on, one immediately wonders which is the chicken and which is the egg," writes Altemeyer.

Ultimately, though, Altemeyer sees fundamentalism as being a "more basic" trait. In other words, the main danger posed by fundamentalists is not necessarily their religious faith but the fact that they "so definitely tend to be authoritarian followers."

Authoritarians tend to exhibit rigid cognition (closed-mindedness), which encourages faulty reasoning. People who believe in a single, inerrant way of life will often twist the facts to fit their worldview. Blogger Larry Allen Brown has condensed Altemeyer's research findings into the bullet points below. In terms of faulty reasoning, RWAs are more likely to:

- Make incorrect inferences from evidence.
- Hold contradictory ideas that result from a cognitive attribute known as compartmentalized thinking, as illustrated by George Orwell's "doublethink."
- Uncritically accept that many problems are "our most serious problem."
- Uncritically accept insufficient evidence to support their beliefs.
- Uncritically trust people who tell them what they want to hear.
- Use many double standards in their thinking and judgments.[99]

Additionally, RWAs exhibit hostility toward out-groups, or people whom they perceive as being unlike them or not sharing their values. For instance, a typical right-wing authoritarian might say, "Take care of your own kind because we are *not* all in this together." Along these lines, RWAs are more likely to:

- Weaken constitutional guarantees of liberty such as a Bill of Rights.
- Severely punish "common" criminals in a role-playing situation.
- Admit they obtain personal pleasure from punishing people.
- Be prejudiced against and hostile toward racial, ethnic, national, sexual, and linguistic minorities.
- Volunteer to help the government persecute almost anyone.
- Be mean-spirited toward those who have made mistakes and suffered.

(Note: Although RWAs are quick to punish "common criminals" and rule-breakers, they are also more likely to look the other way when their leaders break the rules.)

Finally, RWAs are more likely to exhibit the following character attributes:

- Zealous
- Dogmatic
- Hypocritical
- Absolutist

Social dominance, another psychological construct, is closely related to RWA. Developed by Felicia Pratto of the University of Connecticut and Jim Sidanius and UCLA, the social dominance scale measures belief in social *in*equality. People who score high in social dominance do not want a level playing field; they want a hierarchy, and they want to be on top. Social dominators have a desire to rule.

Altemeyer explains that social dominators and RWAs have several things in common: "They both tend to have conservative economic philosophies -- although this happens much more often among the dominators than it does among the 'social conservatives' -- and they both favor right-wing political parties. If a dominator and a follower meet for the first time in a coffee shop and chat about African-Americans, Hispanic-Americans, Jews, Arabs, homosexuals, women's rights, free enterprise, unions leaders, government waste, rampant socialism, the United Nations, and which political party to support in the next election, they are apt to find themselves in pleasant, virtual non-stop agreement. This agreement will probably convince the follower, ever scanning for a kindred spirit who will confirm her beliefs, that she and the dominator lie side by side in the same pod of peas."[100]

However, there are some major differences between RWAs and social dominators, the main one being that dominators crave power. Dominators do not see the world as a scary, sinful realm; they see it as their kingdom to be ruled. Compared to RWAs, they're not as concerned with following the rules. For dominators, rules are meant to be broken. They'll do whatever it takes to get to the top. Whereas right-wing authoritarian tendencies are activated by fears, social dominance is activated by competition. (I have worked with several business school graduates who were groomed to be social dominators and thus live out their lives in a "dog-eat-dog" world.)

While RWAs tend to be religious fundamentalists, social dominators do not. Dominators don't feel bound by a moral code. For them, the end justifies the means. How they play the game is not important; all that matters is that they win.

Altemeyer informs us that "dominators can pretend to be religious, saying the right words and claiming a deep personal belief" and "gullible right-wing authoritarians will go out on almost any limb, walk almost any plank to believe them. So some nonreligious dominators, as a part of the act, do go to church regularly for manipulative reasons."[101]

Social dominators who are also religious fundamentalists are known as "Double Highs" because they score high on the RWA scale as well as the social dominance scale. Altemeyer argues that "a Double High has the best chance of attracting this army of yearning and loyal supporters. He comes packaged as 'one of our own,' one of the in-group. He not only shares their prejudices, their economic philosophy, and their political leanings, he also professes their religious views, and that can mean everything to high RWAs. He too may be faking his religiousness to some extent, but he will have the credentials up front, and the phrase-dropping familiarity with the Bible to pass the test with flying colors. He'll know the code words of the movement. He'll appear to believe everything 'all the good people' believe about Satan, being born again, evolution, the role of women, sex, abortion, school prayer, law and order, 'perverts,' censorship, zealotry, holy wars, America-as-God's-right-hand, and so on."[102]

President Jimmy Carter described "Double Highs" when he observed, "Almost invariably, fundamentalist movements are led by authoritarian males who consider themselves to be superior to others and, within religious groups, have an overwhelming commitment to subjugate women and to dominate their fellow believers."[103]

Now, before you decide that RWAs and social dominators are the enemies who represent everything wrong with the world today, let me remind you that they are people, too, just like you and me. Plus, as Altemeyer points out, RWAs and dominators have their own good qualities as people: "High RWAs are earnest, hard-working, happy, charitable, undoubtedly supportive of people in their in-group, good friends, and so on. Social dominators are ambitious and competitive -- cardinal virtues in American society. It's as big a mistake, I have to keep telling myself, to see people as all-bad as it is to see them as all-good."[104]

We are all products of our environment, and Altemeyer says that this is the "Great Discovery" of social psychology: "Experiment after experiment demonstrates that we are powerfully affected by the social circumstances encasing us. And very few of us realize how much. So if we are tempted by all the earlier findings in this book to think that right-wing authoritarians and social dominators are the guys in the black hats while we fight on the side of the angels, we are not only falling into the ethnocentric trap, we are not only buttering ourselves up one side and down the other with self-righteousness, we are probably deluding ourselves as well."[105]

If we split the world into a dichotomy of all-good and all-evil, then we're making the same fundamental mistake as the fundamentalists. So, the question is: What can we -- those of us who want to be *authoritative* but not *authoritarian* parents -- do to oppose authoritarianism and make the world a better place for our children? We can't argue with the authoritarians; they'll only twist the facts to fit their view. We can't go to war with them because we'd be playing right into their game (and we would probably lose).

What can we do? *We can be their friends.* We can act compassionately and lead by example. We can try to show them that the world is not a scary, evil place, and that people who do not neatly fit into their compartmentalized boxes can in fact be good people, too. In doing so, we might help to reduce some of the very fears that activate authoritarianism and foment violence.

We can also teach our children that trust must be earned, and that even their authority figures should not be trusted automatically. (I wonder how many children have been sexually molested by priests because their parents said that they must always obey and submit to the man with the funny-looking collar.)

We can work together with others in community service projects that matter to everyone. Altemeyer explains the appeal behind this method of outreach: "You're not asking the fundamentalists to come through the door to your side. You're not trying to change their religious beliefs. You're just trying to augment their awareness of others, and increase their Christian charity, by simply giving them the chance to see through an open doorway. Meeting different people in a situation where all are joined in common cause, where all have to work together, can open such vistas."[106]

We can influence the legislative process as voters, candidates, and lawmakers. "You often hear that one cannot legislate brotherhood," Altemeyer writes, "but I think you sometimes can. Anti-discrimination laws, designed to make sure everyone has the rights she is entitled to, can lead many prejudiced people to equal-footing contact with minorities."[107]

The one thing that we shouldn't do is *nothing*.

Altemeyer warns, "The social dominators and high RWAs presently marshaling their forces for the next election in your county, state and country, are perfectly entitled to do what they're doing. They have the right to organize, they have the right to proselytize, they have the right to select and work for candidates they like, they have the right to vote, they have the right to make sure folks who agree with them also vote."[108]

"If the people who are *not* social dominators and right-wing authoritarians want to have those same rights in the future," Altemeyer continues, "they, *you*, had better do those same things too, now. You do have the right to remain silent, but you'll do so at everyone's peril. You can't sit these elections out and say 'Politics is dirty; I'll not be part of it,' or 'Nothing can change the way things are done now.' The social dominators want you to be disgusted with politics, they want you to feel hopeless, they want you out of their way. They want democracy to fail, they want your freedoms stricken, they want equality destroyed as a value, they want to control everything and everybody, they want it all. And they have an army of authoritarian followers marching with the militancy of 'that old-time religion' on a crusade that will make it happen, if you let them."[109]

I don't know if the Callaways would have scored high on assessments for social dominance, but it sure seems like they wanted to control everything and everybody in LaGrange. For nearly a century, they invested their corporate profits in racial segregation and religious fundamentalism, two systems of thought based on the authoritarian power hierarchy. I think it's quite obvious that the Callaways supported social *inequality*. The evidence suggests that they didn't want a level playing field; they wanted a clearly defined hierarchy, and they wanted to be on top, even if that meant violence, disorder, and death for those of us down below.

CHAPTER SIX: PROTO-FASCISM IN AMERICA'S GREATEST LITTLE CITY

"The world will not be destroyed by those who do evil, but by those who watch them without doing anything." - Albert Einstein

Led by a crazed social dominator, authoritarian Nazis exterminated millions of innocent people in their concentration camps before and during WWII. How could this have happened? Might it happen again? These questions loomed large in the years following the war. WWII proved that fascist totalitarianism is not a far-removed, unrealistic threat. Thus, after the war, the authoritarian personality became one of the fastest growing fields of research in the human sciences.

In the Foreword, I referred to the work of Dr. Lawrence Britt, who studied the fascist regimes of Hitler (Germany), Mussolini (Italy), Franco (Spain), and others. According to Britt, there are 14 common, defining characteristics of fascism.

We will examine all 14 characteristics in this chapter, and I will present evidence that what happened in LaGrange in 1935 constitutes an example of a proto-fascism at the municipal level.

But first, let's consider the historical context. In 1935, fascism did not carry the same connotation that it does today. WWII had not yet started, and the world had not been fully exposed the horror spawned by fascist dictatorships in Europe. In fact, at the time, some Americans thought fascism was a darn good idea. For example, the American Fascisti Association and Order of the Black Shirts, "an organization dedicated to the systematic replacement of black workers with unemployed whites," was headquartered in Atlanta, GA.[110] The Black Shirts were most active in 1930, when demonstrators marched down Peachtree Street carrying signs that read: "Niggers, back to the cotton fields -- city jobs are for white folks."

I imagine that several captains of industry also supported fascism in the 1930s. Major General Smedley Butler, who was the most decorated Marine in U.S. history at the time of his death, testified before Congress that a cadre of industrialists had approached him in 1933 and asked him to lead a military coup to overthrow FDR and set up a fascist government in the United States of America.[111]

Now, let's take a look at Dr. Britt's 14 defining characteristics of fascism, listed in bold below: [112]

1. Powerful and continuing expressions of nationalism.

Nationalism involves pervasive flag displays, symbols of unity, jingoistic catch-phrases, and demands for conformity, and it often involves xenophobia (fear of foreigners and outsiders). Hitler was rarely photographed without a swastika in the background or on his person, and his speeches vilified outsiders who were not members of his master race.

Of course, LaGrange is a city, not a nation. Therefore, I'd like to present few examples of what I'll call *municipalism* instead of nationalism. The best examples come from Callaway's PR campaign in 1920. The campaign revolved around the following municipal declaration of conformity: "For the best interests of LaGrange and her people we oppose the organization of labor unions in LaGrange."

In Callaway's campaign, the enemies were outsiders, foreign threats to the hometown: The IWW, the Reds, the Bolsheviks.

"Do you want all these in LaGrange?" the campaign asked. "Well, you will have them as surely as unionism gets a foothold here. The home folks of LaGrange will organize no labor unions. Outsiders will not be permitted to do so."

On February 28, 1935, as the first Callaway Mills strikers walked off their jobs, the *LaGrange Daily News* again blamed radical, outside agitators, while appealing to a desire to protect the hometown from utter destruction:

> There is no finer group of men and women in the textile mills of the United States than the great majority of those living here in LaGrange. The pity of it is that they have been misled by a radical few who have no stake or vital interest in our community. Their action jeopardizes the continuance of the mills of LaGrange . . .
>
> Every worker in the mills who is worthy of the name of a citizen of the community -- every merchant and professional man in LaGrange entitled to call themselves by the name of a LaGrange citizen and every person who values his home, his church, his schools, and the other institutions the community built up through the years must join forces to end that LaGrange mills continue to operate.

Failing in that, LaGrange citizens had just as well fold up their tents, close up their places of business and seek their fortune elsewhere.

Inherent in such threats was the idea that, without Callaway, the city of LaGrange would cease to exist; without Callaway, people's lives would become worthless, and they would be forced to "fold up their tents" and move on to a place that had not been tainted by the outsiders.

2. Disdain for the importance of human rights.

In fascist regimes, rulers cared only about their own rights, and widespread abuses of human rights were justified by dehumanizing the enemy. Propaganda demonized the targets of abuse, while secrecy and denial often covered up the most extreme human rights abuses.

In Fuller E. Callaway's 1920 anti-union campaign, the enemies (union supporters) were vehemently dehumanized. S.H. Dunson wrote that they were "the silent, slimy, and treacherous monster in sheep's clothing," and Callaway described them as the evil common enemy, the plague.

And let's not forget about the ongoing dehumanization of African Americans in LaGrange. The anti-union campaign boasted that its declaration had been "signed by over 4,000 white citizens and heads of families representing every interest in LaGrange."

This type of dehumanization allowed people to perpetrate acts of violence on their fellow citizens. Union supporter W.L. Stroup was kidnapped and beaten, as was Robert Henry, who was left for dead in a ditch. A few years later, Austin Callaway was lynched.

In 1935, the most extreme violence came from state soldiers; this is not surprising since military training programs integrate dehumanization of the enemy. When soldiers killed Fonie Stephens, they probably didn't feel too guilty about it. They were just doing their jobs. In their minds, they didn't kill a fellow human being; they killed the enemy, a troublemaker, a union supporter, a slimy, treacherous monster. By branding union supporters as the common enemy, Callaway also illustrated Dr. Britt's third defining characteristic of fascism:

3. Identification of enemies/scapegoats as a unifying cause.

Blaming "Reds" and "outsiders" for the strikes diverted public attention away from the real reasons for the strikes. In 1920 as well as 1935, LaGrange newspapers warned citizens that outside union organizers just might cause Callaway to gather up his golden eggs and take them elsewhere. Such propaganda was so powerful in shaping public opinion that, after the strike ended, even those who had participated in the strike blamed the unions for the violence and chaos.

4. The supremacy of the military/avid militarism.

When Governor Talmadge declared martial law in LaGrange, National Guard troops used their military might to end the strike. Soldiers established a curfew and told neighbors not to speak to one another. No congregating was allowed. The militiamen carried bayonet-tipped rifles and set up a machine gun in the middle of LaGrange's mill village. The message was clear: Obey and submit to our authority, or else we'll arrest you and send you to the concentration camp in Atlanta, or we'll kill you. Dissent was not tolerated.

5. Rampant sexism.

Propped up by religious fundamentalism, sexism relegated females to the position of second-class citizens. A woman's place was in the home, in the kitchen. Even Fuller E. Callaway's wife was treated like a servant and charged with the duty of managing their home. She received a weekly allowance to cover her expenses, and when she went over that allowance, she had to pay it back to her husband (who had so much money that it's *still* being used to maintain patriarchal systems in LaGrange). Mrs. Callaway knew her place well, it seems.

6. A controlled mass media.

In 1935, mass media in LaGrange consisted of the daily newspaper. Biased, anti-union articles from this period suggest that Callaway had enormous influence if not direct control over what was printed. The day after the strike began, for example, the front page headline was: "Go back to your jobs!"

On March 21, 1935, the *LaGrange Daily News* published an editorial under the following front-page headline: "What Have the Outsiders Done?" Here is an excerpt from the article:

"First and most important is the question, 'WHAT HAVE THE OUTSIDE LABOR AGITATORS DONE FOR THE WORKERS?' Have they brought them greater security? Have they added to the workers' well-being? Have they made it possible for the mills to sell more goods and thus be able to give the people more work? Have they brought money to the workers or have they taken it away? Have they made false promises? What have they done?"

I wouldn't be surprised if that editorial was penned by the same Atlanta-based PR firm that headed up the 1920 anti-union campaign in LaGrange. In addition to the slanted editorials, news articles also exhibited clear bias and framed the union leaders as outsiders. For example, a March 8, 1935 *LaGrange Daily News* article capitalized terms such as "right to work" to emphasize key points: "Strike leaders severely criticize Governor Talmadge for his insistence on the American principle of the RIGHT TO WORK unmolested and unintimidated . . . Union leadership is very smart in many respects but they fail to grasp the temper of America when they revile a Governor of a sovereign state because of his insistence on THE RIGHT OF MEN AND WOMEN TO WORK."

Major newspapers in Atlanta may have been influenced by Callaway's corporate power, too. After the beating of Robert Henry in 1935, for example, Georgia Federation of Labor representative S.A. Hollihan said, "It just doesn't make news for the daily papers of Atlanta."

7. Obsession with national security.

Again, LaGrange is a little city, not a country, but the state military was used to put down the strike under the guise of *municipal* security, and the newspaper praised the National Guard for the "efficient maintenance of peace." Propaganda maintained that it was the outside agitators, not the armed soldiers, who posed a threat to municipal security. In 1920, for example, S.H. Dunson warned that union organization would turn LaGrange into "a veritable Hell on Earth." And let's not forget the centerpiece of the anti-union campaign: a promise of violence, disorder, and death.

8. Religion and ruling elite tied together.

According to Dr. Britt, most fascist regimes "attached themselves to the predominant religion" and "chose to portray themselves as militant defenders of that religion," while the enemies of fascist regimes were often painted as godless heathens.

Fuller E. Callaway put local pastors on his company's payroll, and during the 1920 anti-union campaign, many preachers supported the company's interests. W.P. Cofield, for example, told his congregation at Unity Baptist Church that the "Law of Christ" demanded that industrial workers "respect their obligation to the employer and the community."

Fuller Junior continued his father's tradition by setting up special bank accounts and telling religious leaders, "Let me know when you need more money!" Further, the Callaway Foundation funded 50 percent of the construction costs for all churches built in Troup County for the majority of the twentieth century. There's really no telling how much money the Callaways invested in religion over the years, but it likely adds up to hundreds of millions. Even today, the President of the Callaway Foundation states that their mission revolves around promoting "Christian values."

9. Power of corporations protected.

It's interesting to note that when people in LaGrange talk about "Callaway," it's often impossible to know if they're talking about Fuller, Fuller Junior, Cason, another family member, the defunct textile company, or the Foundation. But it doesn't really matter. Over the years, the name "Callaway" has become synonymous with corporate power. Callaway called the shots in LaGrange; everybody knew that, and many people feared the power behind the name. As Luther Morris, Sr. said in his interview with Mark Langford, "Callaway was boss here. When he said squat, they squatted . . . This was Callaway's town, mister, and don't you forget it. What he wanted to do, he done and got done." When state soldiers rounded up protesters and put them in the military internment camp at Ft. McPherson, they were protecting Callaway's corporate power

10. Power of labor suppressed or eliminated.

Organized labor was the one threat to Callaway's hegemony. Labor power had to be crushed, even if that meant declaring martial law and eliminating the peoples' freedom to gather in public places, leave their houses at night, or even leave their porch lights on at night. Union leaders were beaten, threatened, and demonized as the sole source of the city's problems. And as we'll see in the next chapter, labor power is still suppressed or eliminated in our community.

11. Disdain and suppression of intellectuals and the arts.

Dr. Britt explains that this item really refers to the suppression of *free* expression. Under martial law in LaGrange, people couldn't even freely speak on the street. In her interview with Mark Langford, Ora Woodham said, "If we got out in the daytime, we had to be careful what we said."

Her husband Bill added, "We wasn't allowed to stop and talk on the streets. Just two of us standing and talking to each other, neighbors, friends. We weren't even allowed to speak to each other on the streets." They knew that the soldiers would not tolerate dissent. After Bill's brother made a "cursing remark about the soldiers throwing the stuff out of the house," he was arrested and held at the military internment camp in Atlanta.

Since the strike of 1935, I have to admit that the Callaway Foundation has had a good track record of funding arts and education in LaGrange, but much of this funding has been highly specific. For example, the Callaway Educational Association (CEA) offered various classes in the arts -- but black people were not allowed to set foot on CEA property.

12. Obsession with crime and punishment.

In 1935, union supporters and "troublemakers" in LaGrange were arrested and sent to the military internment camp at Fort McPherson. National Guardsmen patrolled the streets with unchecked power. The two soldiers charged with killing Fonie Stephens were eventually acquitted. The men who beat Robert Henry to the verge of death also got away scot-free. The FBI investigation of Henry's beating was called off, some said, because the Bureau was afraid of offending Callaway.

Today, tall fences topped with barbed wire still surround the old Callaway Mills, many of which are now defunct and abandoned. Full-height turnstiles, also known as "iron maidens," allow just one person at a time to pass through the gates. The old mills look like penitentiary facilities. Were these extreme measures installed to keep outsiders on the outside, or to keep the lintheads on the inside?

13. Rampant cronyism and corruption.

"Cronyism" refers to the practice of placing friends and family members in positions of power. Callaway family members filled several positions of power throughout the history of LaGrange. Fuller E. Callaway's nephew, Dr. Enoch Callaway, testified that Fonie Stephens had died from medical complications, not from the blow to the head he received from the soldiers (even though the medical complications stemmed from the injury to his head). As a result, the two soldiers' who had been charged with Stephens' murder were acquitted.

But Callaway's cronyism extended far beyond the city limits of LaGrange; it went all the way up to the top of our government. As proto-fascism swept across Georgia in 1934-35, President Franklin D. Roosevelt, who had encouraged mill workers to stand up for their rights, was often entertained at Cason Callaway's home.

When WWII broke out a few years later, Callaway Mills received business contracts from the national security apparatus and won several awards from the Army and Navy.[113] Ely Reeves Callaway, Jr., another nephew of Fuller E. Callaway, joined the Army as a Reserve Officer and was posted at the Army's main clothing procurement facility due to his family's textile connections. Ely later founded Callaway Winery and Callaway Golf, manufacturer of the popular Big Bertha golf club. Fuller's grandson (Cason's son) Bo

Callaway also enjoyed the spoils of war. After an unsuccessful campaign bid for Governor of Georgia in 1966, Bo was appointed to the position of Secretary of the Army in 1973. He later served as Chairman of the Republican committee GOPAC.

14. Fraudulent elections.

When Governor Talmadge ran for re-election in 1934, he won the linthead vote by fraudulently claiming, "I will never use the troops to break up a strike." But he had already accepted a $20,000 bribe from mill owners, and as soon as he won election, Talmadge ordered the state's entire National Guard to "arrest the picketers and get the mills back in operation."

Plus, voter disenfranchisement was still standard practice in Georgia at the time. Georgia set up the nation's first poll tax in 1871, which meant that many black sharecroppers (who rarely dealt in cash) were not able to vote. The poll tax cut the state's black vote in half.[114]

***

In this chapter, I have presented some evidence that Callaway corporate power and state military power merged to form a system of proto-fascism in LaGrange in 1935. Perhaps, as I have suggested, FDR failed the working class in some ways by hobnobbing with his pal Cason Callaway instead of intervening on behalf of the workers when state troops marched into the mill villages. On the other hand, as a friend of mine pointed out, successful political leaders must be able to communicate with the wealthy elite as well as the working class. Perhaps FDR learned an important lesson from his careful observation of the ominous situation in LaGrange. In 1938, three years before the United States entered WWII to fight the forces of fascism, FDR pronounced, "The liberty of democracy is not safe if the people tolerate the growth of private power to a point where it becomes stronger than their democratic state itself. That, in essence, is fascism -- ownership of government by an individual, by a group, or by any other controlling private power."[115]

CHAPTER SEVEN: OUR LEGACY

"Be the change you want to see in the world." - Gandhi

The Cotton King divided and conquered by marshalling his vast resources to infect our community with divisive ideologies that reinforce each other in vicious, multi-generational cycles. These divisive ideologies -- racism, sexism, fundamentalism, and authoritarianism -- rest on the common ground of dehumanization. Such ideologies push us to believe that certain people are better than others because of their skin color, gender, spiritual beliefs, appearance, job title, place of residence, or other inconsequential details.

And we did for a long time. Callaway's social engineering project worked like a well-oiled spinning machine for several generations. In 1935, when people started to see through the illusions, break down social barriers, and work together against their oppressor, the Cotton King retaliated by keeping his promise of violence, disorder, and death. State military forces delivered that promise. And on the other side of the Atlantic, Hitler smiled, seeing the fascist movement in Georgia as validation of his own atrocities.

So . . . Where do we stand now? Where do we go from here?

I think we've been divided and conquered for long enough; however, 76 years after the Callaway Mills strike, "union" is still a four-letter word in LaGrange.

Two years ago Kia Motors opened its first American manufacturing facility in West Point, Georgia (a few miles west of LaGrange, near the Alabama state line). Writing in *Dissident Voice*, David McCray reports:

> Astonishingly, prior to its opening in 2009, the Kia plant in West Point, Georgia, had more than 100,000 applications for 2,100 jobs. But in order to keep the union from gaining a foothold (and counter to the law of supply-and-demand), Kia wisely offered high wages and generous benefits. To the folks of West Point, the Kia plant was a godsend, the best manufacturing job anyone had ever seen. Of course, what organized labor -- and, apparently, a few others -- realize is that once the American union movement is more or less neutralized, the economy will not only turn into an extravagant and lopsided sellers' market, the clamps will come down harder and more brutally than anyone could have imagined.

> Without having the unions to use as leverage, the South's oblivious 'free riders' (non-union workers whose wages and benefits are artificially propped up by the existence and threat of the unions) are going to find out exactly what a true 'free market' labor pool looks like, up-close and personal . . . and it ain't going to be pretty.

> Consider: With more than 100,000 applicants fighting and thrashing over 2,100 jobs -- and with no worries or fears about having to compete with union wages and bennies --

why on earth would a company pay more than it was required to pay? Why would a company, any company, part with one nickel more than it absolutely had to?

Without the resistance of organized labor, the law of supply-and-demand will spur an inexorable race to the bottom. And instead of Alabama becoming the New Detroit (as the glossy brochures advertise), it will, in time, resemble the New Bangladesh.[116]

J. Randy Jackson, director of human resources at the Kia plant, said that union representation is a matter for "our team members to decide."[117] Of course, in Troup County, conditions would probably have to deteriorate to the level of those in a Bangladesh sweat shop before the workers would dare to speak of forming a union -- and Kia management knows that. (By the way, ironically, Kia auto workers in South Korea are unionized.)

Some people argue that anti-union attitudes are just as strong throughout the rest of the South as they are in Troup County. I disagree. I think that here in Troup County, because of our secret history of proto-fascism, anti-unionism has a much stronger hold on the conscious and unconscious minds of workers.

Until quite recently, the United Auto Workers (UAW) union had a strong presence in Georgia, even though it's a right-to-work state -- and although Kia management claims that the decision to unionize is up to their employees, they didn't hire a single former UAW member. Julia Bauer reports in *The Grand Rapids Press*:

When Korean automaker Kia decided to build its first assembly plant in the U.S., it chose wide-open spaces on the Georgia-Alabama line, far from big cities and unions, even in those two right-to-work states.

In November [2009], 1,300 newly minted autoworkers began turning out Kia Sorentos for the North American market. Not one of those new employees in the non-unionized plant was pulled from the pool of thousands of unemployed Atlanta-area General Motors and Ford autoworkers.

Their plants had closed down in the shadow of Kia's arrival. Ford's Taurus/Sable plant in Hapeville shut down in 2006, while the Doraville GM plant shut down in 2008.

The GM plant built Monte Carlos, Cutlass Supremes and minivans. At its peak, 5,000 people worked there, and nearly all the hourly employees belonged to the UAW -- even in the longtime right-to-work state where workers cannot be compelled to join as a condition of employment . . .

What galls the Atlanta-area UAW members? The jobs in West Point apparently are off limits to them.[118]

In Troup County, Georgia, our local governing bodies spent a lot of time and money to attract Kia. Local political leaders said that Kia would help our unemployment problem. But unemployment in LaGrange still hovers around 12 percent.

Maybe it's time for the people of LaGrange to stop relying on corporations to save the day. Maybe, despite their rhetoric, corporations really don't give a damn about us. According to some local residents, the Callaway Foundation is *still* more powerful than local government. Maybe that's the real problem. Maybe it's time for us, the citizens of LaGrange, to take back our local government.

At a town hall meeting in September 2011, while drumming up support for a proposed sales tax, LaGrange Mayor Jeff Lukken told citizens that the city plans to restore a particular park that has been closed down for several years (Boyd Park). He said that the City would supply approximately one million dollars out of the five million needed for the project, and the other four million would come from an unnamed private foundation. (Around here, "unnamed private foundation" almost always means the Callaway Foundation.)

Many people wouldn't have a problem with the city accepting $4,000,000 from the Foundation for such a project. After all, LaGrange probably wouldn't be on the map without the infusion of so much Callaway money over the years, right?

But what is the trade-off here? What's at stake? *Is it democracy itself?*

By repeatedly accepting large sums of money from a private corporation, is the City of LaGrange essentially handing over control of the city? Who really runs LaGrange -- the citizens, or the Foundation? Should we just sit back and trust the Foundation to represent our interests?

Let's not kid ourselves! The Callaway Foundation is *not* a purely philanthropic organization. I realize that the Foundation has donated millions of dollars to local hospitals, schools, and churches. (And, as one magazine points out, "even the statue of Lafayette in the heart of LaGrange, which has been the city's symbol since 1976, was created with funds from Callaway's cotton empire."[119]) But ultimately, behind the facade, behind the curtain, behind the board room doors, there seems to be a vested corporate interest that benefits from its influence over local government and development in LaGrange. As long as they have the key to the city, they will probably continue do what's best for their private corporation -- what's best for their own vested interests -- and this may or may not be what's best for the citizens of LaGrange.

Social critic Joe Bageant could have easily been writing about LaGrange when he explained that "the lives and intellectual cultures of the hardest working people" are "purposefully held in bondage by a local network of moneyed families, bankers, developers, lawyers, and businesspeople in whose interests it is to have a cheap, unquestioning, and compliant labor force paying high rents and big medical bills."

Bageant continues, "They invest in developing such a labor force by not investing in (how's that for making money out of thin air!) the education and quality of life for anyone but their own. That means low taxes, few or no local regulations, and a chamber of commerce tricked out like a gaggle of hookers, welcoming the new non-union, air-poisoning factory. 'To hell with pollution! We gonna sell some propity, we gonna move some real 'state today, fellas!' Big contractors, realtors, lawyers, everybody gets a slice, except for the poorly educated non-union mooks who will be employed at the local plant at discount rates. At the same time, and more important, this business cartel controls most elected offices and municipal boards. It also dominates local development and the direction future employment will take."[120]

This isn't democracy! It's "corporatocracy," which psychologist Bruce E. Levine defines as rule by a "partnership of giant corporations, the extremely wealthy elite and corporate-collaborator government officials."[121]

Levine argues that "too many of us have become pacified by corporatocracy-created institutions and culture." He continues, "The elite spend their lives stockpiling money and have the financial clout to bribe, divide and conquer the rest of us. The only way to overcome the power of money is with the power of courage and solidarity."

When we rely on private corporations to build our city parks and carry out other tasks that should be reserved for our local government, do we give up our democratic freedom? Do we relinquish our communal sense of self-reliance and self-determination? Do we forfeit our future and our children's future? Why should we the people of LaGrange rely on the Callaways to cure our city's ills? *Is our local government really that ineffective?*

Georgia singer-songwriter Ken Clark beautifully captures the angst of the working class in LaGrange with his song "Nobody's Strange in LaGrange." Here's a selection of lyrics from the song (available for download at cdbaby.com):

> Please, Mr. Callaway, won't you pay all my bills?
> I will behave myself if you cure all my ills.
> You know, money speaks loudly, but 'round here you can hear it scream!
> Nobody, nobody, nobody's strange in LaGrange...
> Well, we're all just trying to make it
> and fit in with the herd.
> Endangered species should be seen but never heard.
> So we all have to compromise and swallow up our pride
> and deal with the anger that eats us up inside.

Is that really our only option -- to swallow up our pride and deal with the anger that eats us up inside? *No!* History shows that the power of courage and solidarity can overcome corporatocracy, proto-fascism, and even full-fledged fascist dictatorships.

But we have to *want* democracy. We have to want it bad enough to rise up from our recliners and stop watching divisive television programming long enough to examine what's happening in our own city. We have to work together, not against each other. We're all in this together, no matter how hard the powers that be try to divide us. We're all human beings, no matter how hard they try to dehumanize us.

Fuller E. Callaway's father, Rev. Abner Callaway, thought that he *owned* 20 human beings, and he treated them as if they were his property, his chattel. Fuller E. Callaway described his employees as if they were cows, his chattel. When his son Cason took over the mills, he treated the workers like machines, demanding that they "stretch-out" and keep up with the time studies. And so, when Fuller Junior told Chris Boner, "I believe in slavery" -- I think he was being honest. Like his brother, father, and grandfather, he thought of working people as his slaves. He didn't see them as fully human. *Why wouldn't he believe in slavery?*

"You are not machines! You are not cattle! You are men! You have the love of humanity in your hearts!" shouted Charlie Chaplin in his 1930 film *The Great Dictator*, which satirized Hitler's fascist dictatorship. Some have called this speech the greatest ever made. (Search for "Charlie Chaplin final speech in *The Great Dictator*" on YouTube.com to hear the speech in its entirety.) The horrors of WWII revealed the ultimate end of such dehumanization: the herding of people into death camps where they would be murdered by the millions.

Yet a recent news report suggests that the Callaway corporate tradition of dehumanization continues. It seems as if they're still trying to find a way around the Fair Labor Standards Act. Check out the headline:

"Workers Allege 'Slave Labor' at Popular Holiday Display"

The headline refers to the "Fantasy in Lights" Christmas display at Callaway Gardens in Pine Mountain, Georgia. New Leader 9 WTVM reported:

Current and former employees are speaking out about Callaway Gardens' popular holiday lights show, claiming there's a darker side to the sparkling display . . .

Tauna Pierce is the former Wildlife curator at Callaway Gardens. After six years, Pierce resigned from her position in November, tired of what she says are unethical and illegal business practices.

"I feel quite simply that Callaway Gardens has been exploiting their workers. They've been mandating that workers fulfill an 80-hour obligation to a volunteer effort. In my opinion, a volunteer effort is not mandated," she told News Leader 9.

In 2009 and 2010, all salaried Callaway employees were required to take two weeks furlough and put in 80 hours at the five main events the attraction site boasts every year -- the biggest, its "Fantasy in Lights" show.

"It's the Callaway Gardens' slave labor program. What else do you call it when someone forces you to go to a place and provide them profit with your efforts and then not get paid in return? That's indentured servitude maybe if not slave labor."

A current employee who wanted to remain anonymous said this: "It is my hope as a current employee that Callaway's management team isn't taken advantage of as they have been in the past. It's difficult to bring this kind of situation to light because Callaway has created such a culture of fear."[122]

What would it look like if the people of LaGrange came together to send a strong message of solidarity and courage to the Callaways? Such a message might look something like this:

Hey, Mr. Callaway: Working people are not your slaves, and we're no longer afraid of you!

***

On the morning of October 5, 2011, I met with Callaway Foundation President and General Manager Speer Burdette in his office. I explained that I had written a book that's critical of the Foundation, and I wanted to give him a chance to respond to my criticisms.

Burdette is a Certified Public Accountant who grew up in LaGrange and landed his current gig at the Foundation in 2002. Based on my interview with him, he seems like a nice man who truly believes that he is making the community a better place through his work at the Foundation.

I started the interview by asking him about the goals of the Foundation. Burdette told me, "Our mission statement revolves around providing a quality place to live, work, learn, and play in Troup County, promoting that through family Christian values . . . our focus being Troup County -- which is where the money was made that supports the Foundation -- and the improvement of this community in every aspect."

"If you go back in time," he continued, "the Foundation in its foundation was about the support of Callaway Mills. The tax law changed in 1969 and changed in such that a foundation could not own a for-profit business, which, prior to that time, we did actually own the mills. With the sale of the company to Milliken and Company -- of course, that money then came to the Foundation, which then furthered the end uses of the Foundation. But up until probably the last 10 years, we were not quite as focused in Troup County. We had a little more state-wide focus."

Burdette told me about several of the Foundation's philanthropic efforts: They have donated over $300 million since the Foundation was founded in 1943. When the mills were sold to Milliken in 1968, Fuller Junior established Fuller E. Callaway professorial chairs to bring a Callaway professor to every four-year institution in the state of Georgia. It was a $10 million gift to set up as an endowment to provide additional funding to attract the highest level of professors to four-year institutions in Georgia, and it's still active, according to Burdette.

He explained that the Foundation has given tremendous support to Parks and Recreation in Troup County. "If you lived in Atlanta," he said, "it would cost you several hundred dollars to participate, and you'd have to stand in line to be able to participate in anything recreation-wise. In LaGrange, it's $35 to $50 or less. All those facilities pretty much have been provided by the Foundation through the years. We've supported church-building programs. We support the United Way in a big way."

The Foundation also supports the arts. Burdette said, "All of the arts groups in the community, we do support a third of their operating budget."

However, he explained, "We predominately prefer to participate in brick-and-mortar kinds of projects, as opposed to annual budgets, where if we provide the annual budget, then we're always going to have to provide the annual budget."

Over the years, the Foundation has given a lot of money to the Troup County school system, too, primarily for special projects. For instance, Burdette said that each year they fund a field trip to the Georgia Aquarium for every fourth grade student in the system, and they pay to bring in a children's play from Alliance Theatre in

Atlanta. They also fund a local battered women's shelter as well as a homeless women's shelter.

Burdette explained that the officers and staff of the Foundation receive a salary, but none of the trustees receive benefits.

"Mr. Callaway was very proud of the fact that during his entire lifetime, he never received one penny of benefit in any form of fashion from the Foundation personally," Burdette said.

He added, "The only benefit to the Foundation is to see the healthy community we might receive."

At this point, I reminded him that earlier in the interview he had said that the Foundation was started to support Callaway Mills.

"No," he said, "it didn't start to support Callaway Mills. It did in fact support Callaway Mills, but that wasn't the purpose. It started as a philanthropic foundation. It owned the assets of Callaway Mills initially, and it leased those assets back to the mills, and that was the revenue that it used for its charitable purpose."

I proceeded to more specific questions related to the material in this book. I asked, "Why did the Foundation maintain racial segregation at the CEA so long after the rest of the South had moved beyond separate but equal facilities for blacks and whites?"

Burdette replied, "That's just one of those things that continued and realized that it didn't need to go on, and ultimately it changed."

I asked if he thought the continued funding of segregation was related to a corporate effort to maintain a racial divide in the workforce after the strikes in 1934 and 1935.

"Oh, give me a break, that's 50 years later," he said.

I asked, "When was the CEA founded?"

"I don't know," he said. "I don't have any idea, but it's been there for years. I know it was there my whole life -- that's the early

50s. I suspect that the CEA probably was formed around the time of the Foundation or shortly there afterwards. The Foundation was formed in 1943. To try to argue that that was to maintain separate -- now, back in the day -- it was not to maintain -- we were a very racial South. That's the unfortunate truth, and it's taken years of trying to work through that."

I told him I understood that similar practices of segregation occurred all across the South and throughout many mill villages in Georgia. However, I pointed out, "The strange thing about LaGrange is that it lasted until 1993, and that's what's so shocking and, really, the main reason why so many other students, researchers, and professors have encouraged me to do this work and write my book. It's really unheard of that an institution that large and that overtly discriminatory lasted up until the 90s."

"I think it is nothing more than just a continuation," he said. "This is the way it had always been done . . . You know, you had employees of the mills that were both black and white. You know, the mills had sold -- what's that 25 years? [before 1993] -- so certainly no reason to try to anything connected with the mills. I really can't speak because I wasn't there."

I also asked him if he would agree that the Foundation has a long history of supporting religious fundamentalism.

"No," he replied. "We fund all religious organizations. We're non-discriminatory in that respect."

"Would you say that the Foundation has a significant amount of influence over local government and development in LaGrange?" I asked.

Burdette was slower to respond to this question. He chose his words carefully and said, "Yes, but we don't try to exert that influence. We see ourselves more as a resource than a driver. Now, there are some examples, I would give you some examples -- well, maybe we have exerted some influence -- such as in downtown revitalization. We're a resource, but we were an influence there. We believed, again, when we really looked at what we were doing and wanted to focus our dollars on LaGrange and Troup County, that one of the things we needed to do was save the downtown. I mean, all downtowns like ours were dying. The malls had taken away business, and our downtown had become very dilapidated -- a lot of old, empty buildings, so we decided: What can we do about it? So we went out and hired and paid for a lot of planning, and we brought in a lot of planners and urban developers and developed a shred of how it might me and what it might be. We certainly shared it and brought in all of the city. We also brought in community and got input in people from the community as what they thought we should do and how they'd like to see it done, and they came up with a plan, and we've been working that plan ever since. We've been a part of and specifically paid for most of the renovations happening downtown in the last seven or eight years, and I hope you would agree that it's an improvement on where we were."

I nodded my head agreement. It is indeed an improvement.

"We had old buildings," Burdette continued. "We've now got renovated restaurant buildings and a health club and a new movie theater, although we didn't build the movie theater, but we did have the land and make the land available. The parking deck that we've added downtown -- after 6:00 downtown, before, you would've seen nobody, and now you see a pretty good crowd downtown. It's not unusual to go to that parking deck, particularly on a Thursday or Friday or Saturday night, and it might be full. You didn't see any of that five years ago. So, we did take the lead and to some degree exert our influence, but we did it. And of course the city was thrilled for us to do it. We're paying for it, and they thought it was a good plan, and they actually ultimately adopted our plan. Now, that's an instance where we took the lead. Normally, as it relates to government, it would be something that the city might want to do, or the county might want to do, and they'll come to us to assist with funding and ask for our support."

My next question shifted the mood in the room: "In my book I make the accusation that the Foundation does indeed have too much influence over government and development, and because of this is, in fact, a threat to local democracy in LaGrange. The Foundation seems to be a hub of what one psychologist calls 'corporatocracy,' defined as a partnership of corporations, extremely wealthy elite, and corporate-collaborator government officials."

"Well, that's wonderful!" Burdette said. "That is an accusation that I say is absolutely false and unfounded and that you have no basis for saying that, and I'd love to see your research for how you make that statement."

I told him I'd bring in a copy of my book by when I finished it.

"No, no," he protested. "I'd like to see your research, because if you're making statements like that, you're bordering on libel -- because those are false statements. To read it in your book is one thing. I'd like to see your research because if I've missed something."

"I've got one example for you," I told him. "Actually, you gave me a better example -- taking the initiative and exerting the influence over the downtown development -- that kind of thing, in my opinion -- it's a matter of opinion, really . . ."

"Do you think that's bad?" he asked.

"Yes, sir," I responded.

"Wow," he said. "I'd never buy your book." Then he added, "And I don't think your professors believe that's bad."

What an interesting comment! Why would Burdette venture to know what my professors think? Was he insinuating that no professor at a four-year institution in Georgia would be willing to criticize the Callaway Foundation because of the Foundation's donations to every four-year institution in Georgia?

Indeed, author Frederick Hess reports in his 2005 book *With the Best of Intentions*: "Academics, activists, and the policy community live in a world where philanthropists are royalty -- where philanthropic support is often the ticket to tackling big projects, making a difference, and maintaining one's livelihood." Frederick adds that the press "handles philanthropies with kid gloves." One study, for example, looked at press reports on the educational activities of major foundations and found "thirteen positive articles for every one critical account."[123]

Burdette continued, "And I would take you to every downtown planner in the state, and I would take you to the state of Georgia, who has applauded us for that and given us awards for that -- I mean, I really think you've got your head in the sand if that's what you think."

"Can I tell you why I think it's bad?" I interjected.

"Sure," he said.

"That should be reserved for government," I said.

"They'll never do it!" he said. "And we didn't do it without their blessing. I mean, we showed our plan; we shared our plan; they adopted our plan. So, what we did was totally . . . Why don't you go ask the mayor what he thinks about it? Because you're implying that we've imposed something on them. Have you gotten his opinion?"

"I'm pretty sure I know what his opinion is," I said.

"Well, maybe before you make an 'accusation' -- your word -- you might ought to get some facts," he said.

"I've got plenty of facts," I said. "I just wanted to get your opinion."

"I haven't heard a fact," he responded. "I've heard an opinion. I haven't heard a fact."

At this point, feeling the tension rise in the room, I asked, "Do you have anything else that you'd like to add to conclude the interview?"

"No, I'd love to hear some facts," he said. "I mean, you're here asking me, and now you're making accusations. And accusations without facts are dangerous."

Perhaps "accusation" was a poor choice of wording on my part, as it might be taken to refer to illegal activity. Let me be clear: I am not suggesting that the Callaway Foundation is breaking the law in any way. However, in my opinion, the activities of the Foundation constitute a clear threat to our representative democracy in LaGrange.

I pressed on and tried to illustrate my point: "Here's another example: [Mayor] Lukken recently said at a town hall meeting that the city is considering rebuilding Boyd City Park. And he made the statement that the city was willing to invest one million and that a private foundation, which I'm assuming is probably the Callaway Foundation" -- Burdette nodded his head in confirmation -- "would be investing approximately four million to cover the rest of the cost. Now, in my opinion, that's a threat to democracy."

"Why?" he asked.

I explained, "That type of thing, in my opinion, should be reserved for the government and for government funding, not private funding."

"Oh, so we want to raise your taxes to pay for it?" he asked.

"Yes," I said.

"You really do?" he asked.

"Yes, sir," I replied. "That's what government is for."

"Well, you know, I think government is for leveraging opportunities," he said. "And I think government has taken the lead in that [Boyd Park project]. They own the property. Now, the fact that we're assisting in that . . . We gave them the property. That's property that we had originally built, developed, and had given it to the City of LaGrange. Now they're looking at renovating that, and we're willing to assist in that, which was property that we originally built. Now, we have the authority to do that; we have the privilege to do that; it's within our mission to do that; and it's within the law to do that."

He's absolutely right. And since the Citizens United decision of 2010, it's also within the law for for-profit corporations to wield unlimited corporate influence over our elections -- but that doesn't mean it's not a threat to democracy. (President Obama commented on the Citizens United decision, "This ruling strikes at our democracy itself" and "I can't think of anything more devastating to the public interest."[124])

Burdette continued: "And I think most governments would tell you that if they can leverage taxpayer dollars with support from other places, they're being a good steward of the taxpayers' money, and I think that's a perfect example of that. And, gosh, I would strongly disagree with you if you take that other . . . I can't imagine that you would find the support anywhere to say that government -

- that I want to raise more tax dollars so that government does every single thing that might be used by the public. Wow, that's an extreme position."

"I wouldn't disagree with that," I said. I understand that my position may be extreme in the opinion of some.

"But that's the position you just took," he quipped.

"I guess I'm a socialist," I said jokingly. I laughed heartily. He didn't crack a smile.

"Well," he said in a paternalistic tone, "think through the things you're saying. I applaud you for thinking outside the box, but think it all the way through."

I told him that I would take his advice into consideration; that my book was not yet complete; and that it would be thoroughly fact-checked and reviewed by an attorney to make sure that I don't publish anything that is libelous. My goal here is to tell the truth, not to fabricate information. That's why I went to Burdette's office to interview him and allow him to respond to my criticisms of the Callaway Foundation.

"Again, you have the right to express an opinion," he said. "But be clear that this is your opinion. You certainly have the right to do that. Now, I may disagree with you, and that's okay. It doesn't bother me. But if it's your opinion, then state it that way. But don't quote it as fact -- because something like that . . ."

"Really," I interrupted, "what I'm doing with my book is just raising questions and letting other people decide for themselves."

He replied, "If you wanted to raise that as a question -- 'Do you think that this is a proper role for a private foundation?' -- I think that most people would probably respond as I just did. But not everybody."

That's right. *Not everybody.* It turns out that plenty of people see influential private foundations as a threat to democracy. Earl Seals, LaGrange attorney and long-time critic of the Foundation, says that the Callaway Foundation enjoys "representation without taxation." Using tax-sheltered wealth, the Foundation exerts its influence over local government -- and it has much more influence than the average voter. Meanwhile, the average voter must shoulder the tax burden created by the Foundation's tax shelter.

Mr. Burdette might be surprised to learn that some professors do in fact agree with me. Claudio Schuftan, adjunct professor at Tulane School of Public Health, argues that private foundations are "the new plutocracy."[125] ("Plutocracy" means rule by the wealthy elite.)

Joan Roelofs, professor of Political Science at Keene State College in New Hampshire, explains that "the very format [of private foundations] conflicts with radical concepts of democracy" since "foundations are an example of mortmain, the dead hand of past wealth controlling the future."[126]

"Foundation funding carries control over content," Roelofs continues. "It is easier to shape programs begun in the private sector . . . even if they are later adopted by government. By then, the form and content are established, and public agencies generally limit themselves to minor tinkering."[127]

Roelofs also points out that foundation projects are "strongly insulated from popular control." In other words, foundation grants are not subject to political debate. A study from the U.S. Department of Health and Human Services confirms that transparency and accountability are minimal in private foundations, "as there often is a sense that foundation decisions are opaque or even capricious, and that both internal and external accountability measures are minimal."

The researchers add, "While private philanthropists are, in the words of the former president of the Ford Foundation, Susan Berresford, 'managing money that involves a public trust,' they are not accountable to the public in the same sense as [U.S. Government] agencies." [128]

Philanthropist Lewis B. Cullman, who has donated hundreds of millions of dollars to charities in New York, argues that private foundations tend sit on their pots of gold while they should be giving them away to charitable causes. He told *The Wall Street Journal*: "When you set up a family foundation and turn it over to bureaucrats, it is not human nature to vote yourself out. It's time to end that, for the good of all of us."[129]

The *WSJ* article reports: "Mr. Cullman's argument gets to the heart of the different ways Americans donate to charity. Most of us write donation checks directly to needy causes. Those with greater means set up private grant-making foundations, which hold nearly tax-free assets in endowments -- and often give away as little as the government allows. Under current tax law, private foundations are only required to spend 5% of their endowment per year. Twenty percent of that may go to operating expenses. Since endowment investments historically earn more than what they must give out, foundations may never need to dip into their principal assets, yet are able to feed their own administrative bloat in perpetuity."

Those who control foundations leverage the power of the foundation to remain in control, to maintain their spot at the top of the power hierarchy, and to keep others in their place down below. Roelofs explains, "Groups and movements that might challenge the status quo are nudged into line with grants and technical assistance, and foundations also have considerable power to shape things such as public opinion, higher education, and elite ideology. The cumulative effect is that foundations, despite their progressive goals, have a depoliticizing effect."[130]

In her review of *The Revolution Will Not Be Funded*, Kiyoko McCrae writes, "Through foundations, which serve as little more than tax shelters, 'white capital is circulated among white people and works to maintain systems of white supremacy.'"

The perpetuation of the Cotton King's patriarchy, backed by hundreds of millions of tax-sheltered dollars, leaves little room for real democratic engagement or progress in our community. *Foundation knows best. Father knows best. Or does he?*

After I turned off my audio recorder in Burdette's office, he asked me if I was planning to assert that the Foundation had harmed the community.

"Absolutely," I said.

He asked how I could say such a thing since I know about the all of the Foundation's philanthropic activities (and, indeed, since I was a Hatton Lovejoy Scholarship recipient). I reiterated the fact that the Foundation had funded institutional racism up until 1993.

"Don't you agree that this harmed the community?" I asked.

He agreed that it was wrong and that it had lasted for too long, but he seemed unimpressed.

"Put that aside," he said. "Besides that, what else?"

I should have said, *"Isn't that enough?"*

But I gave him another example: "There's also the history of funding religious fundamentalism," I said.

He repeated that the Foundation is proud to support all different types of religious organizations in the area.

"Let me ask you this," he said. "Where do you think LaGrange would be without all the support from the Foundation?"

I told him that LaGrange might not even be on the map without the support of Callaway corporate funding. At that moment, I was reminded of Fuller E. Callaway's 1920 anti-union campaign letter in which he hinted that he would take his golden eggs elsewhere if he did not get his way: "If by any unhappy circumstance LaGrange should be so unfortunate to become union-ridden, I am sure it would mean the death of enterprise in our fair city." I also recalled the warning published on the front page of the *LaGrange Daily News* after the 1935 strike began: "The last resort of the management, we believe, will be closing up and boarding up of the properties."

In a similar vein, Burdette seemed to be suggesting that without the Foundation, LaGrange would be nothing (maybe we should change our bumper stickers to read: "Callaway's Greatest Little City" instead of "America's Greatest Little City"), and without the Foundation's financial support, local government would be totally ineffective. From my perspective, this attitude illustrates how the legacy of paternalism and authoritarianism continues through the Foundation. *Father knows best, and we cannot function without him. It's his way or the highway!*

Later, as I pondered Burdette's question, I realized that LaGrange might actually be a much more vibrant and prosperous city without the historical interference of Callaway's corporate power. Because Callaway actively worked to keep other industries out of the city, there's no telling how many opportunities for growth were blocked by his cotton empire over the years. Without Callaway's influence, LaGrange might currently have a much larger industrial base that would allow workers to collectively bargain for

130

higher pay and better working conditions. Unemployment might not be over 12 percent. The specter of race might not loom so large. Unnecessary violence and death might have been avoided.

What hubris one must have to suggest that others would be nothing without the money he controls!

I also realized this: Callaway would have been nothing without the hard-working people of LaGrange. It was the lintheads who created his wealth. *Without LaGrange, Callaway wouldn't be on the map!*

At the end of our discussion, Burdette and I agreed to disagree. He told me that I have a radical point of view and that if I wanted to reduce private funding of public amenities, then I'd have to change the way government worked.

"I'm working on that," I said, and I handed him my card, which reads: "Vote for Scott Smith, LaGrange City Council."

He promptly handed it back to me and informed me that he wouldn't be voting for me. I thanked him for taking the time to meet with me.

***

As this book started to take shape, I realized that I want to do more than talk the talk (or type the word). I want to give the citizens of LaGrange the option of doing something proactive -- maybe even something radical -- so I decided to step outside of my comfort zone and take a chance. I decided to run for LaGrange City Council. Election Day will be on Nov. 8, 2011. I have no desire to become a career politician, but I want to give LaGrange voters the option for a change, and if I'm elected, I'll work hard to represent the best interests of LaGrange citizens, not the local corporatocracy.

The last municipal election in LaGrange was cancelled because nobody challenged any of the incumbents. This year I'm proud to put my name on the ballot and give voters a choice. As a candidate, I am not accepting any contributions. I believe that campaigns should be based on ideas, not bank accounts and corporate connections. My entire campaign will cost about $500 (because that's all I can afford to spend). Even if I lose the election, I believe that I have already won: My candidacy proves that people don't have to be rich or well-connected to run for City Council. They just have to be residents of LaGrange. If more regular folks don't run for office, the corporatocracy will likely continue to insert their own hand-picked candidates.

In the fall of 2011, as I type these words, thousands of people from across the political spectrum have occupied Wall Street to protest corporate influence in politics. The time is ripe for change. Some have called this is the *American autumn*, referring to the *Arab spring* in which democratic uprisings swept across the Middle East earlier this year. I think it's time for a change at the local level, too.

If the future of our city is up on the auction block, available to the highest private bidder, then maybe the citizens of LaGrange should establish a People's Foundation to counter the influence of the Callaway Foundation. But, wait a minute, isn't that what government is supposed to be? Isn't our government supposed to represent the public interest? Isn't that why we pay taxes?

I remain hopeful that our democracy will triumph. No matter how much money and influence corporate interests may have, we the people still wield the ultimate political power: the power of numbers. However, to tap into that power, we must stand together in courage and solidarity. Is it any surprise, then, that certain corporate interests would invest in social systems that promote fear, dehumanization, and division among the people?

As I look around LaGrange today, I see the repercussions of Callaway's institutional discrimination all around me. Currently, for instance, the City Council consists of three white representatives, all from District 1, and three black representatives, all from District 2. At the 2011 District 2 City Council debates, I was the only white person in the audience besides a reporter from a local newspaper. Racial tension still divides the community on many issues.

However, I have to admit, things appear to be getting better. For example, a group of concerned citizens recently mounted a successful campaign to stop the rezoning of some land in LaGrange's historical district, on Vernon Road near the Callaway mansion. The land in question included a historical home as well as 12 undeveloped acres owned by the Foundation. Developers wanted to tear down the home and build a new medical office building on the land. Nearby neighbors objected, attended City Council meetings, wrote letters to the editor of the newspaper, and even put up yard signs that read: "Save Historic LaGrange!"

And it worked! Ironically, the citizens who campaigned to save their neighborhood were all white, affluent citizens in District 1; however, they didn't receive any support from their District 1 representatives. It was the three African American representatives from District 2 who supported the citizens and ultimately voted down the rezoning bid (at a meeting where one District 1 representative was absent). Since then, the rezoning proposal has been withdrawn, but the developers will most likely try again later.

As I studied this particular issue, I looked at a satellite view of LaGrange on Google Maps, and I realized that, even today, Callaway's stranglehold on LaGrange is visible from the sky. Directly to the west of the land at the center of the rezoning debate, between Vernon Road and Country Club Road, sits a single parcel of undeveloped land. This land at "0 Roanoke Road" consists of 1,266 wooded acres (just over two square miles). The odd thing about this piece of land is that, even though it's in the heart of LaGrange, it has never been annexed as part of the city. Although the city borders this property to the north, south, east, and west, property records list it as "timber land" in "unincorporated Troup County." The records show that the total value of this land is $6,017,210 (and the annual property tax is only $5,233). Why hasn't this piece of land been incorporated into the city?

Troup County property records list the owners of this property as "Ida Cason Callaway Hudson and Philip Cleaveland as trustees." Mrs. Hudson died in 2009, and I can only assume that her husband Charles Hudson took her place as trustee. The other trustee, Philip Cleaveland, served as the last president of Callaway Mills. He has also served on the LaGrange City Council as well as the Callaway Foundation board.

In a 2003 interview, Cleaveland admitted that new development in LaGrange had been blocked by the Callaway Mills Company: "New industry was, frankly, discouraged, and you couldn't find any land. We owned it all! Another thing basically was that we were afraid of unions and were afraid some company would come in here and we'd had enough experience with those after 1934."[131]

I admire Mr. Cleaveland's candor.

"We owned it all!" he said.

After the Callaway mills were sold to Milliken in 1968, the Foundation eventually started selling off plots of land and allowing other industries to set up shop in LaGrange. They no longer "owned it all," but I wonder how much things have changed. According to property records, the Foundation still owns 100+ properties in and around LaGrange. (Note: There are actually two distinct legal entities, the Callaway Foundation and the Fuller E. Callaway Foundation, but for the sake of simplicity, I refer to both as the Callaway Foundation.)

Look at LaGrange on Google Maps, and you will see that the property at "0 Roanoke Road" -- the 1,266 acres of undeveloped woodland -- represents both a predicament and a potential opportunity for our city. Cleaveland reported that the Callaways blocked progress in LaGrange to further their own agenda, and that seems to be happening with this property. The city map shows a slightly disjointed circle that forms the LaGrange bypass. At this time, the circle cannot be completed on the west side of town because it is blocked by the Callaway land. This causes numerous infrastructure problems for the city. Vernon Road, the main east-west corridor which lies to the south of the Callaway land, sees constant traffic problems and is in dire need of repairs. The hospital sits on the far west side of town, and Vernon Road serves as the main route to the hospital. Ambulances need a smooth, clear path. Further, when Hollis Hand Elementary School lets out for the day, traffic grinds to a halt on Country Club Road (which lies to the north of the Callaway land), and there is no way around it. There is no alternate route around that two-square mile piece of land.

This is not a new problem. In 1985, the Georgia Department of Transportation announced plans to widen Vernon Road into a five-line highway.[132] In 1988, the Troup County Board of Commissioners approved a plan which included the relocation of the Callaway mansion gates.[133] Although a portion Vernon Road to the west of the Callaway mansion was eventually widened, the mansion gates were never relocated, and this half-baked solution failed to address the full scope of our city's transportation problems.

We could solve this problem by completing the bypass and extending Broad Street through the middle of the Callaway land to connect with the new portion of the bypass, thereby creating another east-west corridor through town. Look at a map, and you will see that this is the common-sense solution to our transportation problems on the west side of LaGrange.

I've pointed this out to several people, and the general response is: "We can't touch that land! It's Callaway land! We can't do anything about it."

Well, folks, I'm here to tell you that we can do something -- if you want to. If there was ever a justified use of eminent domain, this is it. Eminent domain permits governments to force the sale of private land for public use. Right now, it seems, the Callaways are blocking progress for their own benefit.

Over the past few months, citizens who supported the "Save Historic LaGrange!" effort have stressed the importance of preserving historic landmarks as well as green space on the west side of the city. These enthusiastic citizens succeeded in defeating one rezoning proposal, but the issue will surely return. If the citizens on Vernon Road want to preserve historic LaGrange, now is not the time to sit back and celebrate a small victory. Now is the time to take advantage of the momentum and plan for the future. If people sit back and do nothing, the developers will eventually turn that green space into another asphalt jungle.

If, however, the citizens of LaGrange want to preserve the green space, then now is the time to organize and act. I can think of no better way to preserve the green space than to turn it into a public park with nature trails for walking, jogging, bicycling, and dog-walking. There would be plenty of room for a playground, a dog park, or a small amphitheatre. Imagine all the possibilities! A public park would offer tremendous benefits to all citizens.

If a large enough number of citizens wanted it, they could demand that the city annex the Callaway land and employ eminent domain to not only complete the bypass but also develop a beautiful city park that preserves the natural green space and buffers the historic district from new development. This is a rare opportunity; most municipalities don't have two square miles of undeveloped green space in the heart of the city. I should note that eminent domain is normally used a last resort. In most cases, a compromise prevails before a forced sale. However, the people of LaGrange need to know that the option of eminent domain can be used for *leveraging opportunities*.

Imagine what might happen if, through a show of solidarity and courage, the citizens of LaGrange stood up to Callaway corporate power for the first time in 76 years.

Unfortunately, many people seem to be resigned to the following attitude: "I can't do anything about that. How could I possibly make a difference?" I've also heard people blame our political and economic problems on "cultural" factors, as if nothing can be done about it, as if *we just have to wait for culture to change on its own.*

Do we? Culture is a set of behavioral norms. As individuals and groups change, people change culture. We have the ability to change ourselves and to affect (and effect) change at the cultural level. Plus, as Americans, we live in a democratic society where (almost) every adult can vote.

How can we change culture? On an individual level, we can closely examine our history, our environment, and our attitudes. We can ask ourselves: *Where did these attitudes come from? Do they make sense? Could I develop healthier, more compassionate attitudes?*

At the group level, we can change our culture by voting and participating in the political process. Far too many people don't exercise this fundamental right. Imagine what might transpire if more informed citizens went to the polls.

＊＊＊

As I type the final words in this book, my wife and I are preparing for the birth of our first child. *What kind of father will I be?* I wonder. *What will be my legacy?*

I hope that I will be an *authoritative* but not *authoritarian* father -- *paternal* in the fatherly sense, but not *paternalistic* in the patriarchal sense. Paternalism, according to the World English Dictionary, is "the attitude or policy of a government or other authority that manages the affairs of a country, company, community, etc., in the manner of a father, especially in usurping individual responsibility and the liberty of choice."[134]

I hope that, as a father, I will be able to teach my son about responsibility by giving him the freedom of choice -- not by usurping his responsibility and liberty with the message that *might makes right, so it's my way or the highway!* My greatest strength as a father may be my realization that father doesn't know best. Mother, father, and child must collaborate to discover what's best.

I hope that our son will grow up in a city where citizens demand unfettered democracy and accept the responsibility that comes along with that freedom, instead of allowing private corporate interests to take the reins. Such private interests often claim that we would be nothing without them. "They'll never do it!" said Callaway Foundation President Speer Burdette, referring to our local government's inability to build public facilities without the support of the Foundation. Is our local government really so pathetic? Are we the people really so apathetic? I would hope not.

The private corporate interests at the top of the hierarchy want us to sit back and let them run our government for us. They want us to keep kissing their asses while they promise to deliver more free money. They want us to fight amongst each other while they chart our children's future.

They don't want us to take back our democracy. They don't want us to know about our community's secret history, and they certainly don't want us to know about the option of eminent domain. But now we know. So, what now?

Some people have scoffed at my ideas and called me an idealist. If believing in democracy makes me an idealist, then I'm guilty as charged. Where would America be without the idealists who continued to share their dreams in the face of fierce opposition?

The idealists who founded the U.S.A. certainly changed their culture. We can change our culture, too, but we have to start with ourselves. As Gandhi said, we have to be the change we want to see in the world. It's not easy, but it's possible.

It's up to you.

What will be *your* legacy?

AFTERWORD

Writing this book has been an eye-opening but sad, sobering experience. I'm glad that I wrote it, but I'm also glad to be done with it. This book is essentially a rough draft. I could've probably spent another 10 years researching and writing, but I wanted to get this feverishly-written manuscript into your hands as soon as possible. You never know what tomorrow may bring. Plus, I want the people of LaGrange to understand why I am running for City Council before Election Day arrives on Nov. 8.

The primary goal of this book is to begin a dialogue. I'd love to hear from you, whether you agree or disagree with my ideas. What do you think? Can we change our culture here in LaGrange? How? Share your comments at: **www.LegacyLaGrange.com**

REFERENCES

[1] Proceedings of the First Industrial Conference. October 6 to 23, 1919. Government Printing Office, Washington: 1920. p. 73. Accessed online: http://books.google.com/books?id=mzwuAAAAYAAJ&printsec=frontcover&source=gbs_ge_summary_r&cad=0#v=onepage&q&f=false

[2] Lightle, Bill. *Mill Daddy: The Life and Times of Roy Davis*. Mill City Press: Minneapolis, 2009.

[3] Benito Mussolini quotes. ThinkExist.com. Accessed online: http://thinkexist.com/quotes/benito_mussolini/

[4] Winant, Gabriel. "The Revolution the South Forgot." *Salon*. Sept. 7, 2010. Accessed online: http://www.salon.com/news/politics/war_room/2010/09/07/southern_labor_history.

[5] "Welcome." Callaway Foundation, Inc. Accessed online: http://www.callawayfoundation.org/cfi_entry.php.

[6] "Callaway Family." The New Georgia Encyclopedia. Updated 08/17/2009. Accessed online: http://www.georgiaencyclopedia.org/nge/Article.jsp?id=h-2915.

[7] "Callaway Educational Association Records." Troup County Archives. Accessed online: http://www.trouparchives.org/index.php/manuscripts/entry/manuscript_ms-115/.

[8] Scott, Carole E. "Chief William McIntosh." Accessed online: http://freepages.history.rootsweb.ancestry.com/~cescott/parks/chief.html .

[9] "William McIntosh." The New Georgia Encyclopedia. Updated 08/27/2009. Accessed online: http://www.georgiaencyclopedia.org/nge/Article.jsp?id=h-3541

[10] Hurt, R. Douglas (2002). *The Indian Frontier, 1763-1846 (Histories of the American Frontier)*. Albuquerque: University of New Mexico Press.

[11] Worthy, Larry. "North Georgia Creek History." *About North Georgia*. Accessed online: http://ngeorgia.com/history/creekhistory.html.

[12] "The Trail of Tears." *About North Georgia*. Accessed online: http://ngeorgia.com/history/nghisttt.html.

[13] "Samuel Slater and Moses Brown Change America." Brunswick Junior High School curriculum. Accessed online: http://www1.brunswick.k12.me.us/bjh/depart/curric/nationgrows/virtualtelegraph/periods/period1/slaterbrownreport.htm.

[14] "Callaway Family." The New Georgia Encyclopedia. Updated 08/17/2009. Accessed online: http://www.georgiaencyclopedia.org/nge/Article.jsp?id=h-2915.

[15] Whitley, Donna Jean. "Fuller E. Callaway and Textile Mill Development in LaGrange, 1895-1920." Ph.D. dissertation, Emory University, 1984: 4.

[16] Whitley, 5.

[17] Whitley, 16.

[18] Whitley, 18.

[19] "Callaway Family." The New Georgia Encyclopedia. Updated 08/17/2009. Accessed online: http://www.georgiaencyclopedia.org/nge/Article.jsp?id=h-2915.

[20] Ingram, John M. (1983). "Fuller Earle Callaway." Biographical dictionary of American business leaders, Volume 1. Westport, Connecticut: Greenwood Press. Accessed online: http://books.google.com/books/about/Biographical_dictionary_of_American_busi.html?id=qzxy3pejsdoC.

[21] Wood, Carleton. "Cotton Farming, Mill Villages and Fancy Parterres: The Woven Landscapes of LaGrange, Georgia." *Magnolia*. Summer-Fall 2008.

Accessed online:
http://www.southerngardenhistory.org/PDF/Magnolia_summerfall2008.pdf.

[22] "Fuller E. Callaway, LaGrange, GA." Textile Industry History: Textile Titans.
Accessed online: http://www.textilehistory.org/FullerECallaway.html.

[23] Whitley, iv.

[24] Proceedings of the First Industrial Conference. October 6 to 23, 1919.
Government Printing Office, Washington: 1920. p. 72-76.

[25] "A Spectator at the Industrial Conference." *The Review*. A weekly journal of
political and general discussion. Volume 1. From May 17, 1919, to December 31,
1919. Part II. The National Weekly Corporation. NY. p. 587. Accessed online:
http://books.google.com/books?id=YY5NAAAAYAAJ&printsec=frontcover&source
=gbs_ge_summary_r&cad=0#v=onepage&q&f=false.

[26] History and Heritage. Callaway Foundation. Accessed online:
http://www.callawayfoundation.org/history.php.

[27] Callaway, Fuller E. Letter to Mr. Huff, City Auditor. Nov. 29, 1916. Troup County
Archives. MS9.

[28] Irons, Janet. (2000.) *Testing the New Deal: The General Textile Strike of 1934 in
the American South*. University of Illinois: Chicago, 26.

[29] LaGrange Chamber of Commerce Advertisement. 1920. Troup County Archives.
MS9.

[30] Whitley, 293.

[31] Whitley, 306.

[32] Whitley, 300.

[33] Whitley, 297.

[34] Whitley, 304.

[35] Whitley, 315.

[36] Whitley, 292.

[37] Whitley, 308.

[38] "Linthead." UrbanDictionary.com. Accessed online: http://www.urbandictionary.com/define.php?term=linthead.

[39] "The New Deal." Clairmont Press. Accessed online: http://mystatehistory.com/georgia/ga_05/ch_11_3.pdf.

[40] Irons, 3.

[41] Irons, 48.

[42] Irons, 136.

[43] Lorence, , James J. *The Unemployed People's Movement: Leftists, Liberals, and Labor in Georgia, 1929-1941*. 2009. University of Georgia: Athens, 105.

[44] Lorence, 122.

[45] Winant, Gabriel. "The Revolution the South Forgot." *Salon*. Sept. 7, 2010. Accessed online: http://www.salon.com/news/politics/war_room/2010/09/07/southern_labor_history.

[46] Lorence, 115.

[47] Irons, 143.

[48] Lorence, 111.

[49] Lorence, 106.

[50] Lorence, 116.

[51] Langford, Mark. Interview with Bill Woodham, LaGrange, 1988. Troup County Archives.

[52] Langford, Mark. Interview with Jesse Maddox, LaGrange, 1988. Troup County Archives.

[53] Irons, 159-160.

[54] "Ask Talmadge to Send Troops: Textile Workers and Public Officials Make Request for Callaway Mills." *The Spartanburg Herald*. March 5, 1935. p. 1. Accessed online: http://news.google.com/newspapers?id=pkUsAAAAIBAJ&sjid=rcoEAAAAIBAJ&pg=4539,328127&dq=callaway+mill+strike&hl=en

[55] "Memorandum on Beating of Robert Henry, Union Member, La Grange," Oct. 19, 1935, Stetson Kennedy Papers, Atlanta, Georgia State University, Pullen Library, Southern Labor Archives, Box 1514.

[56] Lorence, 11.

[57] Lorence, 157.

[58] Lorence, 14.

[59] Lorence, 229-231.

[60] Beacham, Frank. "Chiquola Mill shooting hits 75-year mark." Belton and Honea Path News-Chronicle. September 6, 2009. Reprinted by Dave Tabler at Appalachian History. Accessed online: http://www.appalachianhistory.net/2010/08/the-shooting-at-chiquola-mill-became-known-as-bloody-thursday.html.

[61] Langford, Mark. Seminar Paper Interviews, LaGrange, 1988. Troup County Archives.

[62] Neuman, W.L. (2006.) *Social Research Methods: Quantitative and Qualitative Approaches*. Sixth Edition. Boston, MA: Pearson Education, 95.

[63] Gladwell, Malcolm. (2005). *Blink: The Power of Thinking without Thinking*. Back Bay Books: New York, NY.

[64] Hatfield, EA. "Segregation." Georgia Encyclopedia. Updated 11/06/2009. Accessed online: http://www.georgiaencyclopedia.org/nge/Article.jsp?id=h-3610&hl=y.

[65] Alexander, Michelle. (2010.) Speaking at Demos February 18, 2010. Youtube video: "Michelle Alexander: Drug War Racism." Accessed online: http://www.youtube.com/watch?v=lgM5NAq6cGI

[66] "Along the NAACP Battlefront." *The Crisis*. p. 324. October 1940. The Crisis Publishing Company. Accessed online:

http://books.google.com/books?id=7FoEAAAAMBAJ&printsec=frontcover&sourc
e=gbs_ge_summary_r&cad=0#v=onepage&q&f=false.

[67] Whitley, 42.

[68] Whitley, 43.

[69] Lewis, Jone Johnson. Gloria Steinem Quotes. About.com. Accessed online:
http://womenshistory.about.com/cs/quotes/a/qu_g_steinem.htm.

[70] Winant, Gabriel. "The Revolution the South Forgot." *Salon*. Sept. 7, 2010.
Accessed online:
http://www.salon.com/news/politics/war_room/2010/09/07/southern_labor_his
tory.

[71] Baker, Don. (2010.) "Understanding Right Wing Authoritarianism." Atheist
Experience #477. Atheist Community of Austin. Accessed online:
http://www.youtube.com/watch?v=cWlj5hN6SM4.

[72] Weaver, Frank G. "Do you know the kinship between a potted geranium and
cotton cloth? What Fuller E. Callaway Discovered." Young Men's Christian
Association magazine. September 1919. p. 480. Accessed online:
http://books.google.com/books?id=KjPmAAAAMAAJ&printsec=frontcover&sourc
e=gbs_ge_summary_r&cad=0#v=onepage&q&f=false.

[73] History and Heritage. Callaway Foundation. Accessed online:
http://www.callawayfoundation.org/history.php.

[74] Oral History with Charles Hudson, Sept. 17, 2003. Interview by Mike Moncus.
Troup County Digital Archives Project. Accessed online:
http://project.thclibrary.net/oralhistory/docs/charles_hudson.txt.

[75] DiDonato, Nicholas C. (2011.) "Religion and intolerance." Exploring the nexus of
culture, mind and religion. Accessed online:
http://www.ibcsr.org/index.php?option=com_content&view=article&id=347:relig
ion-and-intolerance&catid=25:research-news&Itemid=59.

[76] Jones, James W. (2006.) "Why does religion turn violent? A Psychoanalytic
Exploration of Religious Terrorism." *Psychoanalytic Review*. 93(2): 169. Accessed
online:
http://www.psybc.com/pdfs/library/Why_Does_Religion_Turn_Violent.pdf

[77] Jones, 168.

[78] Jones, 170.

[79] Jones, 186.

[80] "Last words of a terrorist." (2001.) *The Observer*. September 30, 2001. Accessed online: http://www.guardian.co.uk/world/2001/sep/30/terrorism.september113.

[81] Jones, 180.

[82] "Judgment Journey 2008." Posted on YouTube.com by mswrcr29. Accessed online: http://www.youtube.com/watch?v=o_4yFHYQFsg.

[83] Jones, 171.

[84] Jones, 179.

[85] Larsen, Stephen. "(2007.) The Fundamentalist Mind: How Polarized Thinking Imperils Us All." The Theosophical Publishing House: Wheaton, IL. Accessed online:
http://books.google.com/books?id=3tGNTcQlMZwC&printsec=frontcover&source=gbs_ge_summary_r&cad=0#v=onepage&q&f=false, 215.

[86] Newberg, Andrew & Waldman, Mark Robert. (2010). *How God Changes Your Brain: Breakthrough Findings from a Leading Neuroscientist*. p. 18. New York: Ballantine.

[87] Newberg & Waldman, 27.

[88] Newberg & Waldman, 28.

[89] Newberg & Waldman, 45.

[90] Newberg & Waldman, 48.

[91] Newberg & Waldman, 110.

[92] Newberg & Waldman,, 144.

[93] Pigott, Robert. "Dutch rethink Christianity for a doubtful world." August 5, 2011. BBC News Europe. Accessed online: http://www.bbc.co.uk/news/world-europe-14417362.

[94] Hedges, Chris. (2006.) American Fascists: the Christian right and the war on America. Free Press: New York, NY. Accessed online: http://books.google.com/books?id=BusC7zEgyVgC&printsec=frontcover#v=onepage&q&f=false

[95] http://www.asap-spssi.org/pdf/asap023.pdf

[96] Altemeyer, Bob.(2006.) *The Authoritarians*. p. 8. Accessed online: http://members.shaw.ca/jeanaltemeyer/drbob/TheAuthoritarians.pdf.

[97] Altemeyer, 15.

[98] Mavor, K. I., Louis, W. R., & Laythe, B. (2011). Religion, prejudice and authoritarianism: Is RWA a boon or bane to the psychology of religion? *Journal for the Scientific Study of Religion*, 50(1), 22-43.

[99] Brown, Larry Allen. "Right Wing Authoritarianism: What is the allure in being a follower?" Accessed online: http://larry-allen-brown.suite101.com/right-wing-authoritarianism-a61455

[100] Altemeyer, 168.

[101] Altemeyer, 166.

[102] Altemeyer, 189.

[103] Altemeyer, 187.

[104] Altemeyer, 228.

[105] Altemeyer, 237.

[106] Altemeyer, 248.

[107] Altemeyer, 250.

[108] Altemeyer, 253.

[109] Altemeyer, 250.

[110] Lorence, 39.

[111] McCormack-Dickstein Committee. (1934.) U.S. House of Representatives, Special Committee on Un-American Activities, Investigation of Nazi Propaganda Activities and Investigation of Certain Other Propaganda Activities by United States Congress. Wikisource. Accessed online: http://en.wikisource.org/wiki/McCormack%E2%80%93Dickstein_Committee#Public_Statement_on_Preliminary_findings_of_HUAC.2C_November_24.2C_1934.

[112] Britt, Laurence W. (2004.) "Fascism anyone?" *Free Inquiry Magazine*. 23(2). Accessed online: http://www.secularhumanism.org/index.php?section=library&page=britt_23_2.

[113] Wood, Carleton. "Cotton Farming, Mill Villages and Fancy Parterres: The Woven Landscapes of LaGrange, Georgia." *Magnolia*. Summer-Fall 2008. Accessed online: http://www.southerngardenhistory.org/PDF/Magnolia_summerfall2008.pdf.

[114] Anderson, E. and Jones J. "Race, Voting Rights, and Segregation: Direct Disenfranchisement." The Georgraphy of Race in the United States. University of Michigan. Accessed online: http://www.umich.edu/~lawrace/disenfranchise1.htm.

[115] "Anti-Monopoly." *Time*. May 9, 1938. Accessed online: http://www.time.com/time/magazine/article/0,9171,759590,00.html.

[116] Macaray, David. "Are we losing our last, best hope?" *Dissident Voice*. April 7, 2011. Accessed online: http://dissidentvoice.org/2011/04/are-we-losing-our-last-best-hope/.

[117] Hirsch, Jerry. "Who wants a union? Not Southern autoworkers, it seems." *Los Angeles Times*. March 29, 2011. Accessed online: http://articles.latimes.com/2011/mar/29/business/la-fi-0329-autos-unions-20110329/2.

[118] Bauer, Julia. "Laid-off UAW workers galled that they can't get jobs at non-union Kia plant." Grand Rapids Press. Sept. 12, 2010. Accessed online: http://www.mlive.com/news/index.ssf/2010/09/laid-off_uaw_workers_galled_th.html.

[119] Wood, Carleton. "Cotton Farming, Mill Villages and Fancy Parterres: The Woven Landscapes of LaGrange, Georgia." *Magnolia*. Summer-Fall 2008. Accessed online: http://www.southerngardenhistory.org/PDF/Magnolia_summerfall2008.pdf.

[120] Bageant, Joe. (2007). *Deer Hunting with Jesus: Dispatches from America's Class War*. p. 28. Crown Publishers: New York.

[121] Levine, Bruce E. "10 Steps to Defeat the Corporatocracy." AlterNet. May 20, 2011. Accessed online: http://www.alternet.org/economy/151018/10_steps_to_defeat_the_corptocracy/.

[122] Connell, Lindsey. "Workers allege 'slave labor' at popular holiday display." News Leader 9 WTVM. Dec. 20, 2010. Accessed online: http://www.wtvm.com/Global/story.asp?S=13716668.

[123] Barkan, Joanne. "Got Dough? How Billionaires Rules Our Schools." *Dissent*. Winter 2011. Accessed online: http://www.dissentmagazine.org/article/?article=3781.

[124] Stolberg, Sheryl Gay. "Obama turns up heat over ruling on campaign spending." The New York Times. Jan. 23, 2010. Accessed online: http://www.nytimes.com/2010/01/24/us/politics/24address.html.

[125] Schuftman, Claudio. "Private foundations are the new plutocracy." *The Broker*. Sept. 20, 2011. Accessed online: http://www.thebrokeronline.eu/Blogs/Bellagio-Initiative/Private-foundations-are-the-new-plutocracy.

[126] Roelofs, Joan. (2003). *Foundations and public policy: the mask of pluralism*. p. 20. State University of New York Press: Albany, NY.

[127] Roelofs, 23.

[128] Person, Ann E., et. al. (2009). "Maximizing the value of philanthropic efforts through planned partnerships between the U.S. government and private foundations: literature review." Mathematica Policy Research, Inc. Accessed online: http://aspe.hhs.gov/hsp/09/philanpart/appendixb.shtml#_Toc224033436.

[129] Panero, James. "The Best Way to Really Give Away Money." Wall Street Journal. August 20, 2010. Accessed online: http://online.wsj.com/article/SB10001424052748704554104575435481403466748.html.

[130] Roelofs, back cover.

[131] Oral history interview with Philip Cleaveland, May, 12, 2003. Interviewed by Mike Moncus. Digital Library of Georgia. Accessed online: http://dlg.galileo.usg.edu/meta/html/trou/oralhist/meta_trou_oralhist_p_cleaveland.html.

[132] "DOT to Detail Vernon Road Widening Plan." *LaGrange Daily News*. July 11, 1985.

[133] "County Approves Vernon St. Widening." *LaGrange Daily News*. August 3, 1988.

[134] "Paternalism." World English Dictionary. Dictionary.com. Accessed online: http://dictionary.reference.com/browse/paternalism.

Made in the USA
Charleston, SC
29 December 2011